TAROT

TAROT

GEDDES & GROSSET

Published in this edition 2005 by Geddes & Grosset

© 2005 Geddes & Grosset,
David Dale House, New Lanark, ML11 9DJ, Scotland

ISBN 1 84205 534 8

Printed and bound in Poland

POLSKABOOK

Contents

Introduction

The exact origins of Tarot are unknown. It seems that the earliest records of its existence show that it was first known as a card game with the French title *Les Tarots*, which was played in Italy. This game, still played today in some countries, bears no resemblance to the current practice of using Tarot cards for the purpose of divination.

The Tarot pack was used solely in card games for some considerable time. It was not until the late eighteenth century that it seems to have become connected with the practice of divination. Nowadays Tarot cards are used mainly by people who are trying to predict the future, although they are also sometimes used as an object of focus by people who are practising meditation.

A great many theories exist as to the origins of Tarot cards, linking them to different cultures and beliefs. One of these theories is that Tarot originated from Egyptian hieroglyphics. The connection between Tarot and the Egyptian culture was explored by a French intellectual of the eighteenth century, Court de Gebelin. While working on a vast study of the occult, he developed the theory that there existed a link between Tarot and 'the Book of Thoth', Thoth being the Egyptian god of science. Trismegistus, a Greek alchemist and teacher of magic, is supposed to have set down his teachings in this 'book'. The popularity of this theory can be accounted for by the great interest in all things Egyptian at the time.

In the mid-nineteenth century the work of Court de

Gebelin was developed by Alphonse Louis Constant, another Frenchman with an interest in the occult. He developed a system for interpreting Tarot cards that inspired the printing of several Tarot decks.

Another theory concerning the origins of the Tarot cards is that the Knights Templar set down their beliefs in the twenty-two cards of the Major Arcana. It is held that this was done just before the dissolution of the Knights Templar and the execution of the Grand Master, Jacques du Molay, in 1314. Although there are several Christian elements in Tarot cards, any connection between the Knights Templar and the introduction of Tarot cards is thought to be unlikely.

Other suggestions regarding the origins of Tarot are that it was brought to Europe from Asia by gypsies, that it is of Arabic origin and crusaders brought it back with them, or that it is of Indian origin and a very early form of chess. There do seem to be very close connections between the Tarot and the Cabbala, which is an ancient Jewish practice of mysticism and magic. The mystery of the origins adds to the magic and individual interpretation of the cards today.

Whatever the true origin, Tarot as we know it today, has its root in the early Renaissance period of history. The earliest surviving Tarot cards are Italian and were made for the Visconti family in Milan around the year 1450. These are sometimes known as the Bembo cards after the artist, Bonifacio Bembo, who is usually credited with painting them for the Visconti family. Not everyone believes that Bembo was the person who was responsible for the making of the cards, and some people ascribe their creation to Francesco Zavattari.

Many of the cards that are regarded as being histori-cal and genuine are French, not Italian, in their design. Of these, the Tarot de Marseilles which is pictured in this book is well known. In the seventeenth century the manufacture of Tarot cards in northern Italy more or less stopped. Cards were then imported into Italy from France.

Tarot cards have altered and developed over the cen-turies. The Colman Smith-Waite pack is not the same as the Tarot de Marseilles, and in turn the Tarot de Mar-seilles is not the same as the Visconti pack. Some of the earliest packs had more than seventy-eight cards, and the order of the cards has changed several times.

In the late twentieth century Tarot has become widely popular as people have become fascinated by New Age practices and a desire to know what the future holds in these uncertain times. Once, those interested in the oc-cult were regarded with suspicion, but now the produc-tion of occult books and decks of Tarot cards is big busi-ness. There are a great many sets of Tarot cards to choose from – even Salvador Dali produced a Tarot pack as one of his works. The decks that exist vary in their sym-bolism. Some draw inspiration from ancient civilisations, such as that of the Celts, and some are based on fantasy. All the packs that exist are beautifully designed and can be appreciated as works of art in their own right. In-deed, a great many of the Tarot decks that are sold will never be used for the purpose of divination.

There is often quite a lot of mystique and ritual relat-ing to the use of Tarot cards, perhaps because of the great amount of ancient symbolism attached to them. Many users of Tarot cards feel that they must keep their cards wrapped in a piece of black or purple silk, and many then place the silk-wrapped pack in a home-made wooden box.

Some believe that a Tarot pack should never be bought by the person who is going to use it. They feel that to have maximum effectiveness a Tarot pack should be purchased by someone else and given to the intended user as a gift.

Many users of Tarot do not like people other than themselves or their clients touching their cards. They feel that they have built up a special symbolic relationship with their cards which will be destroyed by someone else's touch.

Several users of Tarot like to observe certain rituals when they are giving a reading. They may like, for example, to burn incense or play music. Others may open a reading by saying a prayer. Some may feel that they have to be in a particular part of the room, facing in a particular direction.

A Tarot pack consists of 78 cards altogether, 22 of which form the Major Arcana. The Major Arcana cards are more significant than the cards of the Minor Arcana as they symbolise major changes in the querent's life. Each card has a number, and this is also significant when doing a reading as the recurrence of a particular number in a reading has its own significance. The numbers are:

Fool	0
Magician	1
Lady Pope or High Priestess	2
Empress	3
Emperor	4
Pope or Hierophant	5
Lovers	6
Chariot	7

The other 56 cards form the Minor Arcana and are split into four suits: Wands (sometimes referred to as Sceptres, Rods, Batons or Staves), Cups, Swords and Coins (sometimes referred to as Pentacles or Discs). Each suit has ten numbered cards (for example, the Eight of Coins) and four court cards. The court cards are the Page, the Knight, the Queen and the King.

The Minor Arcana cards are said to have associations with today's playing cards, and those interested in the art of cartomancy may find that there are similarities in the interpretations of cards. Below are the suits of playing cards and their suggested antecedents:

Wands	Diamonds
Cups	Hearts
Swords	Clubs
Coins	Spades

Each suit of the Minor Arcana has its own significance

and symbolism. Minor Arcana cards symbolise the thoughts, feelings, actions and desires that allow changes to occur in the querent's life. The numbered Minor Arcana cards can be dominated by the court cards and the Major Arcana cards, so their interpretation will be influenced by the other cards in the reading. The interpretation of a reading will also be influenced if one suit is strongly represented. For example, if in a Celtic Cross spread three of the cards were from the suit of Cups it would indicate the prominence of the querent's emotional circumstances.

Wands

Wands are associated with thoughts, inspirations, desires and the identifying of goals. Although other terms exist, Wands is the most favoured as it captures the sense of magic and spiritual power associated with the suit. Wands indicate that the querent has ambitions and thoughts that may create change in the future.

Cups

Cups are associated with emotions, feelings and spiritual experiences. Cups indicate that the querent will be preoccupied with relationships and spiritual experiences. There is a focus on being rather than on doing.

Swords

Swords are associated with action, conflict and struggle. Swords indicate that the querent will be involved in arguments and disputes, and although this may at first appear to be negative it can be very positive. Swords can indicate that stagnant situations will change and ill feeling be brought out into the open.

Coins

Coins or pentacles are associated with the realisation of goals, material wellbeing and rewards for hard work. Coins indicate a prosperous time for the querent, but it is important to remember that material wellbeing and spiritual health do not always go hand in hand.

Using Tarot Cards

Choosing a Tarot Deck

When buying a deck of Tarot cards it is important to look at all the different types of cards that exist and to study them. The individual should choose a deck that he or she is attracted to and appreciates.

Storing Tarot Cards

Some people believe that the way in which Tarot cards are stored is very important. Experienced users often keep their decks wrapped in black or purple silk and placed in a box so that the power of the cards' energies will not be altered or weakened. Experienced divinators will often not let others touch their decks or will ensure that this is kept to a minimum. If you go to a professional Tarot reader, you will probably be allowed only to cut the deck and will not be asked to shuffle the cards. This practice keeps the individual bond between the divinator and his or her pack, which allows for intuitive interpretations of readings.

First Steps in the Practice of Divination

1. On purchasing a deck of cards, the querent should hold each card and familiarise himself or herself with the card and its interpretations. The bond will grow stronger with time, and more intuitive interpretations will be the result.

2. Before beginning a reading, the querent should formulate the question he or she wishes to ask and repeat it aloud.
3. While shuffling the cards the querent should meditate on the question being asked but think of nothing else.
4. The querent and divinator should not allow preconceived ideas to enter the mind during the process.

The Significator

The first step is to select a significator card, which represents the person making the query (the querent) or the matter about which the inquiry is being made. The court cards of the Minor Arcana are the cards to choose from to act as significators:

King of Wands   a fair-haired or auburn-haired man over forty years of age with blue eyes and a fair complexion.

Queen of Wands   a fair-haired or auburn-haired woman over forty years of age with blue eyes and a fair complexion.

Knight of Wands   a fair-haired or auburn-haired man under forty years of age with blue eyes and a fair complexion.

Page of Wands   a fair-haired or auburn-haired woman under forty years of age with blue eyes and a fair complexion.

King of Cups   a man over forty years of age with light brown hair and grey or blue eyes.

Queen of Cups   a woman over forty years of age with light brown hair and grey or blue eyes.

Knight of Cups   a man under forty years of age with light brown hair and grey or blue eyes.

Page of Cups	a woman under forty years of age with light brown hair and grey or blue eyes.
King of Swords	a dark-haired man over forty years of age with hazel or grey eyes and a dull complexion.
Queen of Cups	a dark-haired woman over forty years of age with hazel or grey eyes and a dull complexion.
Knight of Cups	a dark-haired man under forty years of age with hazel or grey eyes and a dull complexion.
Page of Cups	a dark-haired woman under forty years of age with hazel or grey eyes and a dull complexion.
King of Coins	a swarthy-skinned man over forty years of age with very dark hair and eyes.
Queen of Coins	a swarthy-skinned woman over forty years of age with very dark hair and eyes.
Knight of Coins	a swarthy-skinned man under forty years of age with very dark hair and eyes.
Page of Coins	a swarthy-skinned woman under forty years of age with very dark hair and eyes.

The above significators are based on physical attributes alone, and if these do not seem appropriate it is possible for the person doing the reading to choose a more suitable card based on character traits. It is also possible that the significator card can reflect the nature of the inquiry. For example, if the querent wants to know if a legal action is likely, the Justice card of the Major Arcana could be used as the significator.

The Celtic Spread

The significator having been selected, it should be placed on the table facing upwards. The significator card will be under card number one in the diagram.

The querent should then shuffle and cut the rest of the pack three times, keeping the cards facing down and meditating on the inquiry that is being made.

Then the querent should turn over the **first card** of the pack and lay this card over the significator. This card is card number 1 in the diagram on page 23. This card should be interpreted as signifying the influences affecting the querent and the general atmosphere.

Then the querent should turn over the **second card** in the pack and lay it across card number 1. This card should be interpreted as symbolising the nature of the obstacles that stand in the way of the querent.

The querent should then turn over the **third card** and place it in the position above cards number 1 and 2. This card should be interpreted as representing the querent's aim or ideal in relation to the inquiry or the best that can be achieved under the circumstances but that has not yet happened.

The querent should then turn over the **fourth card** and place it in the position below cards number 1 and 2. This card should be interpreted as representing the foundation or basis of the matter, that which has already happened.

The querent should then turn over the **fifth card** and place it to the right of cards number 1 and 2. This card should be interpreted as representing that which is happening or has just happened.

The querent should then turn over the **sixth card** and place it to the left of cards number 1 and 2. This card should be interpreted as representing the future and that which is ahead of the querent.

These cards are now positioned in the shape of a cross, and the following four cards should be placed in a line from bottom to top to the right of the cross formation.

The querent should then turn over the **seventh card** and place it at the bottom of the line to the right of the cross. This card should be interpreted as representing the position or attitude of the querent in the circumstances.

The querent should then turn over the **eighth card** and place it above card number 7. This card should be interpreted as signifying the environment and influences of the querent.

The querent should then turn over the **ninth card** and place it above card number 8. This card should be interpreted as identifying the querent's hopes and fears.

Finally, the querent should turn over the **tenth card** and place this above card number 9. This card should be interpreted as representing the final result, the culmination that is brought about by the influences of the other cards in the reading.

The spread is now complete, but should card number 10 be a difficult card to draw a final decision from, or if it does not have any obvious association with the inquiry, it would be wise to repeat the reading using the tenth card as the significator instead of the one previously used. In this case the pack must again be shuffled and cut three times before the ten cards can be laid out as before.

If the tenth card is a court card, it indicates that the matter of the inquiry rests in the hands of the character represented by the court card. It is possible to achieve a greater understanding of the motivation and nature of this character by doing another reading using the court card as the significator.

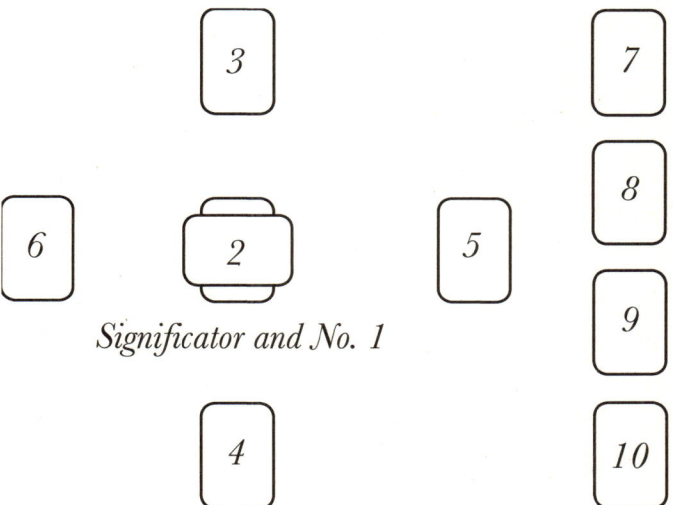

Significator and No. 1

An Alternative Method

First, the querent should shuffle the entire pack and turn some of the cards round so that they are in the reversed position. The querent should then cut the pack with his or her left hand.

The querent should then deal out the first forty-two cards into six piles, each containing seven cards. The cards should be facing upwards, and the first seven cards dealt should form the first pile, the next set of seven cards should form the second pile, and so on until all forty-two cards are dealt. The end result should be like that in the diagram on the next page.

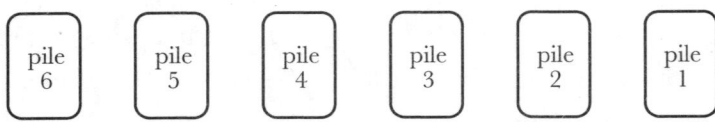

The querent should then pick up the first pile of cards and lay the cards in a row from right to left, as below:

The querent should then pick up the second pile of cards and place the cards on top of the cards of the first pile in the same order as before.

The querent should repeat this process until all the piles have been dealt out and seven new piles exist, as below:

The querent should then take the top card of each new pile and shuffle them, then lay them out from right to left making a line of seven cards.

The querent should then take the next two cards from each pile and shuffle them together before laying them out in two lines of seven cards under the existing line.

Next the querent should pick up the remaining twenty-one cards and shuffle them before laying them out in three lines of seven cards below the existing three lines. The result should be that the querent has six lines of seven cards arranged in horizontal lines, as shown on page 25.

In this method the querent is represented by the Magician if the querent is male and by the High Priestess if the querent is female. The significator card should not be taken from the pack until after the forty-two cards

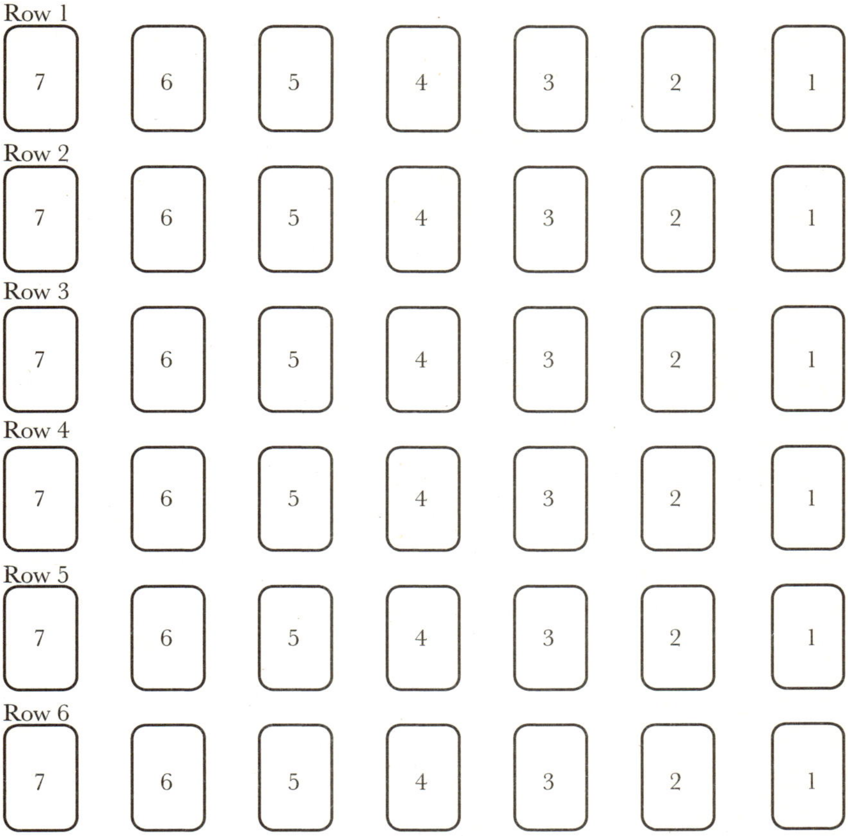

Row 1

| 7 | 6 | 5 | 4 | 3 | 2 | 1 |

Row 2

| 7 | 6 | 5 | 4 | 3 | 2 | 1 |

Row 3

| 7 | 6 | 5 | 4 | 3 | 2 | 1 |

Row 4

| 7 | 6 | 5 | 4 | 3 | 2 | 1 |

Row 5

| 7 | 6 | 5 | 4 | 3 | 2 | 1 |

Row 6

| 7 | 6 | 5 | 4 | 3 | 2 | 1 |

have been laid out. If the Magician or High Priestess card is not among the cards laid out in the spread it will be found in the remaining thirty-six cards and should be placed a little to the right of the first horizontal line. If, however, the card is found among the forty-two cards it should be removed and placed as before. In this case another card should be randomly selected from the remaining thirty-six cards to fill the space.

The querent should then read the cards in succession from right to left, beginning at card number 1 of the top line at the extreme right. Therefore, the last card to be read will be the card at the extreme bottom left.

This spread is the most suitable when the querent does not wish to ask a specific question but does want some general guidance regarding his or her life and destiny. The querent can give general outlines such as the period of time he or she wishes to know about. However, these specifications should be made at the beginning of the process and concentrated on for the duration.

The Simple Spread

In this spread only three cards are drawn. One can represent the past, another the present and another the future. It is best if you have a specific question to ask your three cards and you should decide what they signify beforehand. They could also represent the situation, the problems surrounding it and the outcome. To choose these cards it is probably easiest to shuffle them and spread them all out in front of you, choosing the three cards to which you are most drawn.

To understand the past ask the question: "Which events have I experienced that affected my situation as it is now?" as you pick the first card and place it face down. To understand the present ask the question: "What is the truth about my current situation or attitude?" as you choose the second card and place it next to the first, also face down. To understand what the outcome will be, choose the last card while asking the question: "What will the outcome of my situation be?" and place the last card face down next to the second. Further cards can be chosen if, for example, you need further guidance or advice as to how to avoid an unfortunate outcome.

Advice for Interpreting Tarot Readings

The person interpreting the cards (the divinator) should remember that the interpretation of the cards must be made relevant to the querent and the question asked. The official and conventional meanings of the cards should be adapted to harmonise with the particular case in question – the position, time of life, and sex of the querent. The general trend of the cards should also be taken into consideration, and the divinator should allow intuition to play its role.

At the beginning of the reading the divinator should briefly run through the cards laid out to get a general impression of the subject – the trend of the destiny – and then read each card in detail.

The divinator should try to refrain from letting personal opinions interfere in the reading of the cards as this will alter the interpretation. It is obviously difficult to do this if one person is both the querent and the divinator, but it is important if a true reading is to be gained.

The Major Arcana

The Fool, Le Mat, Il Pazzo, El Loco

0

The Fool

Pictorial Symbolism

The card shows the figure of a young man dressed in fancy clothes. His gaze is cast above him. Although the figure here is stationary, it is obvious by his stance and the bounding of the dog behind him that he has no intention of stopping. Where there is a precipice in the design of this card, as in the A E Waite/Pamela Colman Smith cards, he shows no fear of the depths below him. It is as if he believes that if he should fall he will be caught and saved by angels. He is striding onwards on his journey. He appears to be in a dreamlike state. In the Marseilles deck he carries a walking stick, which is a symbol of materiality, and a pouch, by which he is weighed down. The fool is on a journey through the material world, burdened, but naively carrying on as if he has no cares. The contents of the bag he carries are linked to the items seen on the table of the magician or juggler card which in turn are linked to the suits of the minor arcana.

Divinatory Meaning

The Fool card is 0 and is considered to represent the beginning of a spiritual journey. The Fool can represent the child in us. There is a focus on trust and hope, but this could reflect uncertainty on the part of the querent. It highlights the uncertainties of life but also that sometimes it is necessary to take an apparently risky step to make good, and at other times that it is wiser to stay put. This card's presence in a reading indicates to the querent that it is important to trust his or her judgment and plan for the future but to do so wisely. This is not a good time to make binding commitments. The Fool card represents trust, ideals, hope of a bright tomorrow, choice and folly. Even if the experiences lead to failure they do not represent true danger

Reversed Meaning

When the Fool card appears in the reversed position in a reading it represents negligence, absence, carelessness, apathy and vanity. The querent may be feeling eccentric at this time and be inclined to extravagant behaviour, but this could lead to his or her downfall.

Special Consideration

The Fool card is very much open to interpretation by the querent. The other cards in the reading may well give the querent more clarity.

The Magician, The Juggler, The Magus, Le Bateleur, Il Bagatto, El Mago

I

The Magician

Pictorial Symbolism

In the Marseilles deck the magician is shown performing some sleight of hand with some of the objects of his trade on the table before him. In some versions of the cards the juggler, or magician, has on the table the implements that can be found in the suits of the tarot: a dagger (swords), a cup, a pentacle, and a wand in his hand. In the Marseilles pack, dice, baubles, cups and other trinkets are found rather than the suit symbols. These are primitive versions of the symbols of the minor arcana. In Pamela Colman Smith's cards the pentacle is included on the magician's table and above the magician's head is a figure of eight on its side, which symbolises infinity and the closed circle of energy. In that design there is a serpent encircled round the figure's waist and devouring its own tail symbolises eternity. The picture in this deck depicts a representation of the energies of the universe. In the card pictured here a bag sits upon the juggler's table, this same bag could be seen to be carried by the Fool. His burden is the symbolic contents of the tarot.

Divinatory Meaning

The presence of a Major Arcana card will dominate a reading and will carry more weight than Minor Arcana cards. The Magician card is number one, and ones in a reading indicate a new beginning and change. There is a focus is on new beginnings and acting to realise one's desires. The Magician card represents skill, diplomacy, subtlety, self-confidence and will. These are all traits that the querent needs to draw on in order to be able to achieve his or her goals. However, the querent should exercise some caution as the Magician card can also represent treachery. The querent may feel manipulated and exploited by another. In this situation the querent should meditate and follow his or her instincts.

Reversed Meaning

When the Magician card appears in the reversed position in a reading it represents disgrace, self-deceit, lies and misuse of power. The querent may be involved in a tricky situation and either the querent or another is lying in order to shift the blame.

Special Consideration

When the Magician card appears in a reading the querent must pay extra attention to the surrounding cards as they hold the key to what is beginning and why. The querent must then follow intuition in order to find the best course of action.

The High Priestess, La Papesse, The Lady Pope, The Papess, La Papessa

II

The Lady Pope

Pictorial Symbolism

In the Marseilles pack, La Papesse, or The Lady Pope represents woman, the meeting of spirituality and materiality, and contemplation. The design is thought by some to have been based on the legend of Pope Joan, said to have ruled in the guise of a man as Pope John VII in 853 AD – until she gave birth in the street. Historians have been unable to verify her existence. Behind her head is a double wimple which some have thought suggests horns, thus she has been identified with the horned goddess Isis, Egyptian goddess of rebirth and archetypal symbol of feminine power. Her stance, seated on a throne with open book, is one by which artists have depicted Isis. Some claim she has no connection with the Pope Joan legend but rather she is a symbol of the Church or the Papacy itself. In Pamela Colman Smith's design the High Priestess figure is seated between two pillars, one dark and one light, which indicate balance. These are thought to correspond to the double wimple of the Marseilles card. The High Priestess card symbolises the feminine force. It represents mystery and magic, which is shown in the Colman Smith design by the presence of a scroll inscribed with 'Tora', signifying the greater law and the second sense of the world. The open book on her knee in the Marseilles deck is a symbol of knowledge and ideas and the search for these.

Divinatory Meaning

The presence of a Major Arcana card will dominate a reading and will carry more weight than Minor Arcana cards. This card is number two, and twos in a reading indicate a period of gestation, of waiting and anticipation of great success in the future. There is a focus on waiting, gathering knowledge, and balance. The High Priestess card represents wisdom, mystery, understanding, gathering strength, intuition and serenity. It indicates a time of gestation before goals can be realised but also indicates the importance of using this time wisely to acknowledge inner changes and wait until one's energies are released. During this time of waiting the querent will quietly be gathering strength and knowledge that will prove useful in the future.

Reversed Meaning
When the High Priestess card appears in the reversed position in a reading it represents ignorance, conceit, surface knowledge and an immoral nature.

Special Consideration
The presence of this card indicates that the querent is troubled by the future and that this is causing problems. The High Priestess card symbolises truth and indicates that the future will be positive as the querent has new strengths to draw on.

The Empress, L'Imperatrice

The Empress

Pictorial Symbolism

In the Marseilles deck, the Empress sits upon a throne, holding in her left hand a sceptre and in her right a shield emblazoned with an eagle. At her back appear to be two wings – actually part of the throne she sits upon, but symbolically she does have wings because she represents the soul of Everyman and our wish to 'fly', to develop and grow. In the Colman Smith cards you can see how the symbolism has been adapted as the Empress represents earthly paradise and shows a Venus-like figure in a field of corn with a waterfall behind her. The Venus symbol in the picture shows that she is a representation of womanhood and motherhood. The twelve star cluster shows that her role is a universal one as these represent the twelve constellations of the zodiac.

Divinatory Meaning

The presence of a Major Arcana card will dominate a reading and will carry more weight than Minor Arcana cards. The Empress card is a number three, and threes in a reading suggest the involvement of more than more than one person and can also indicate that there will be a period of suspended activity before future successes. There is a focus on being rather than doing, on being in tune with one's inner feelings and emotions. The Empress card represents fruitfulness, feelings, emotions, development, creativity and fertility. The Empress card indicates that the querent will be rewarded as a result of fruitful labour. The querent should not be disillusioned by delays but trust his or her instincts and there will be success in the future.

Reversed Meaning

When the Empress card appears in the reversed position in a reading it represents idleness, ignorance, inaction and waste. The querent may feel uncertain at this time and may experience difficulties in expressing himself or herself. This will not last and is only a temporary state.

Special Consideration

The Empress card is a card that represents the emotions and indicates to the querent the importance of following instincts and feelings. The querent should not be redirected by thought and action.

The Emperor, Sovereign, L'Empereur

IV

The Emperor

Pictorial Symbolism

The Emperor card represents a powerful figure resting cross-legged against a throne. If you follow the curve of his back to his crossed legs in this rather awkward looking pose, the design looks somewhat like the symbol for Jupiter, ♃. He is clothed in a manner that shows his power. The eagle on his throne is a symbol of power too and relates to the eagle on the shield of the empress. The staff that he holds in his right hand represents a wand, indicating his power in the spiritual world. In the Colman Smith design the corners of his throne are fronted by two rams' heads, indicating an association with the astrological sign of Aries.

Divinatory Meaning

The presence of a Major Arcana card will dominate a reading and will carry more weight than Minor Arcana cards. The Emperor card is number four and fours in a reading indicate the realisation of one's goals. There is a focus on definite changes that will be obvious in the querent's life. The Emperor card represents strength, dominance, stability, power, authority, will, conviction and protection. The emperor card indicates that this is a time when new opportunities will present themselves to the querent, and if these opportunities have solid foundations they should bring the querent success. The querent should act promptly, without delay, but should allow for changes and be willing to make adaptations accordingly.

Reversed Meaning

When the Emperor card appears in the reversed position in a reading it represents immaturity, impulsiveness, obstruction and hastiness. The querent may be wasting a great deal of energy at this time by acting without thought and causing arguments.

Special Consideration

There is little spiritual guidance to be interpreted from the Emperor card as it is a very practical card with its roots in this world.

The Pope, Le Pape, Il Papa, The Hierophant, The High Priest

V

The Pope

Pictorial Symbolism

The Pope or Hierophant is seated on a throne – a different throne from that on which the Emperor sits. His throne indicates his power over the spiritual world. There are religious connections represented in this picture. The Pope holds a triple-cross sceptre in his left hand. The seven points of the sceptre are associated with the seven deadly sins of Christianity. He is frequently regarded as representing the pope or the head of the church. At his feet two figures are kneeling, showing respect and servitude to their teacher. These two figures are likely to represent the querent, seeking knowledge

Divinatory Meaning

The presence of a Major Arcana card will dominate a reading and will carry more weight than Minor Arcana cards. The Pope card is number five, and fives in a reading indicate a time of changes and a period of ups and downs. There is a focus on the querent's relationships with others, groups and individuals. The querent is striving to find the truth and make sense of the changes in his or her life. The card represents conventionality, captivity, servitude, marriage and alliance. This card shows the querent the importance of commitments to others and the strength of relationships. If the querent has concerns about a relationship, the presence of this card indicates that he or she should persevere and continue to work on the relationship.

Reversed Meaning

When the card appears in the reversed position in a reading it represents weakness, gullibility, the need for tolerance and understanding. The querent may be involved with an individual whose behaviour is irritating and self-indulgent. However annoying this person is, the best course of action is for the querent to show tolerance.

Special Consideration

The querent should be inspired to achieve greater spiritual understanding by clearing his or her mind of feelings and thoughts that belong in the past.

The Lovers, L'Amoureux, Gli Amanti, The Crossroad

The Lovers

Pictorial Symbolism

In the Marseilles deck a young man stands between two women, as if having to make a choice between them. Above, cupid flies, encompassed by the rays of the sun, waiting to shoot an arrow towards the three. The two women perhaps symbolise opposing elements. The male figure in the middle is symbolic of the querent, whether the querent is a man or a woman. In this design one woman is beautiful, the other is ugly. In the Colman Smith design, the Lovers card shows two figures – one male and one female. Their nudity suggests youth, innocence, love and purity. Comparisons can be made to Adam and Eve. The winged figure in the background represents Cupid. The trees behind the figures are the Tree of Life and the Tree of Knowledge. This card is simpler in symbolism than the Marseilles design and is a representation of human love.

Divinatory Meaning

The presence of a Major Arcana card will dominate a reading and will carry more weight than Minor Arcana cards. The Lovers card is number six, and sixes in a reading indicate adaptability and the ability to change in times of difficulty. There is a focus on love, relationships and change. The Lovers card represents attraction, love, beauty, romance, harmony and trials overcome. This card indicates to the querent that a new relationship will be successful and of deeper significance than previously experienced. If the querent is already involved in a relationship, this card shows that any problems will be overcome and that old bonds are still strong. The querent should be wary of taking things at surface value and should be aware that situations that appear to be negative may well come good in time.

Reversed Meaning

When the Lovers card appears in the reversed position in a reading it represents failure, the break-up of a relationship, frustration and division. The querent may experience difficulties in a relationship, which will result in insecurity. However, the relationship may be salvaged providing that both parties wish it to be so.

Special Consideration

This card is very much concerned with fate and divine power. It shows that the querent should keep faith in order to prosper.

The Chariot, Le Chariot, Il Carro

The Chariot

Pictorial Symbolism

The male figure of The Lovers card has now been transformed into a charioteer. The figure symbolises control and conquest on all planes. Although he is a princely figure, he is not a member of a priesthood. Therefore the conquests that he has made are manifest or external and not within himself. He does not hold the answer to spiritual questions. The horses that pull the chariot represent emotions, but they seem to be pulling in different directions. The horses also show that the card is ruled by the sign Sagittarius

Divinatory Meaning

The presence of a Major Arcana card will dominate a reading and will carry more weight than Minor Arcana cards. The Chariot card is number seven, and sevens in a reading indicate a time of solitude and of questioning oneself. There is a focus on identifying problems by asking oneself searching questions while heeding the importance of learning lessons from previous mistakes. The Chariot card represents change, providence, triumph, problems overcome and troubles. The key to the Chariot card is to take control of a situation while remembering the importance of compromise. Once the querent has identified the cause of the problem, all aspects of his or her life will begin to progress and improve.

Reversed Meaning

When the Chariot card appears in the reversed position in a reading it represents litigation, dispute, defeat, quarrelling and failure. The querent may find at

this time that it is easy to become involved in arguments over petty matters. One such argument could
lead to litigation, which would result in the querent
being defeated.

Special Consideration
The Chariot card represent the storm before the calm.
It is a powerful card that promotes immediate action.
The querent should be alert and try to remain in control
in order to succeed.

Justice, La Justice, Justicia

VII

Justice

Pictorial Symbolism

The figure in the picture is seated between two pillars – in a similar position to that of the High Priestess. The pillars of justice open on one world and the pillars of the High Priestess onto another. In this instance the pillars open onto the world of spiritual and moral justice. The card of Justice symbolises the scales, and the sword indicates a balance of mercy and retribution. The card indicates that decisions have to be made, and options weighed up.

Divinatory Meaning

The presence of a Major Arcana card will dominate a reading and will carry more weight than Minor Arcana cards. The Justice card is number eight, and eights in a reading are very positive and indicate positive changes. There is a focus on fortitude and courage. The querent should be true to convictions and challenge those who are in the wrong. The Justice card represents power, energy, action, courage, success and balance. This is a very positive card, which should motivate the querent to have faith in himself or herself. The Justice card in a man's spread indicates a female to whom he will be attracted. It is clearly associated with the sign Libra and indictes that there are options to be decided.

Reversed Meaning

When the Justice card appears in the reversed position in a reading it represents legal complications, bigotry, bias and excessive severity. The querent's behaviour may have been excessive of late, and this may result in repercussions, perhaps in the form of a fine.

Special Consideration

The Justice card indicates to the querent the importance of achieving a balance within oneself as well as in one's surroundings. This cannot be rushed, however, and time must be allowed to run its course.

The Hermit, L'Hermite, L'Eremita

VIII

The Hermit

Pictorial Symbolism

The figure in the picture is dressed in ancient robes and carries a lantern. This represents the blending of the idea of the Ancient of Days with the Light of the World. The beacon that the figure holds intimates 'where I am, you may also be'. In simple terms the Hermit is searching for something

Divinatory Meaning

The presence of a Major Arcana card will dominate a reading and will carry more weight than Minor Arcana cards. The Hermit card is number nine, and nines in a reading indicate the completion of events. There is a focus on an important situation in the querent's life. The querent may well be about to progress on to a new stage of life but needs to remove any difficulties from the current situation in order to be able to make the progression. The querent may have recently experienced difficulties that resulted in loneliness and isolation. Once the querent feels that this situation is entirely in the past, he or she will be able to help others experiencing similar difficulties. The Hermit card represents wisdom, prudence, solitude, faith and discrimination. This card indicates that the querent is self-aware and this self-knowing will prove useful in achieving greater wisdom and understanding.

Reversed Meaning

When the Hermit card appears in the reversed position in a reading it represents a lack of faith, unreasoned caution, concealment and a closed heart and mind. The querent may be feeling a desire to be detached from those close to him or her, but the motivation is wrong and the action is cold-hearted.

Special Consideration

The Hermit card indicates to the querent the need to face up to imperfections. It is necessary to come to terms with and accept these in order to allow development. The querent should strive to divest himself or herself of thoughts of distrust and reservation.

Wheel of Fortune,
La Rove de Fortune

X

The Wheel of Fortune

Pictorial Symbolism

The wheel depicted on the card symbolises the flux of human life and the perpetual motion of the universe. The crowned creature holding a sword symbolises the equilibrium and stability amid movement.

Divinatory Meaning

The presence of a Major Arcana card will dominate a reading and will carry more weight than Minor Arcana cards. The Wheel of Fortune is number ten and therefore a one $(1 + 0 = 1)$. Ones in a reading indicate a new beginning and change. There is a focus on potential success following changes in the querent's life. The Wheel of Fortune represents destiny, fortune, success, elevation, luck and change. The presence of this card in a reading indicates to the querent that it is important to let things run their natural course. The querent would be well advised to make few plans as these may well have to changed. This card indicates that the key to success is adaptability. The changes that occur in the querent's life will be of a positive nature.

Reversed Meaning

When the Wheel of Fortune appears in the reversed position in a reading it represents bad luck, uncertainty and decline. The querent may find that changes occurring in one area of his or her life have a negative effect on another area. In order to identify which area may suffer, the querent should pay close attention to the other cards in the reading as they will hold the answer.

Special Consideration

Out of chaos a new start will emerge for the querent. The other cards in the reading are especially obtaining an exact interpretation of the significance of the Wheel of Fortune. The other cards will determine the direction and influence of the change.

Strength, Fortitude, La Force

XI

Strength

Pictorial Symbolism

The picture shows a young woman forcing open (or is it closed?) the jaws of a lion, demonstrating her power over nature. It can be seen that the lion is already calmed and tamed by the nature of the woman . In the Colman Smith design the woman is leading th lion by a chain of flowers. The lion signifies passions, and she who is called Strength is the higher nature in its liberation.

Divinatory Meaning

The presence of a Major Arcana card will dominate a reading and will carry more weight than Minor Arcana cards. The Strength card is number eleven and therefore a two (1 + 1 = 2). Twos in a reading indicate a period of gestation, of waiting and anticipation of future success. There is a focus on matters concerning the law or partnerships. The Strength card represents control, determination, courage and change. The presence of the Strength card indicates to the querent that if he or she is involved in a legal dispute the hearing will be just and fair, and the outcome will probably favour the querent.

Reversed Meaning

When the Strength card appears in the reversed position in a reading it represents weakness, discord, disgrace and lack of faith. The presence of this card suggests that disharmony has resulted from the abuse of power, leaving others resentful and bitter.

Special Meaning

The Strength card in a reading should inspire the querent

to face up to situations that may appear to be difficult. This will develop the querent's confidence and self-esteem and help him or her to retain his or her sense of purpose.

The Hanging Man, The Hanged Man, Le Pendu

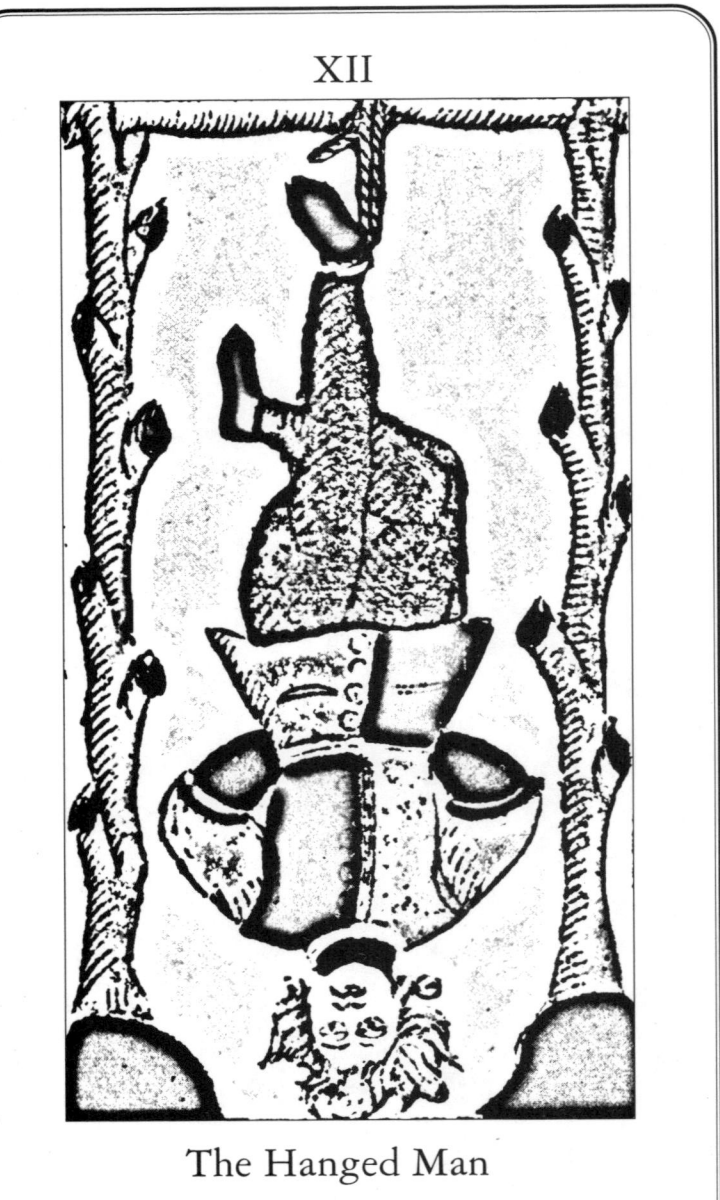

The Hanged Man

Pictorial Symbolism

The figure is suspended from a cross while his body also forms a cross. The Hanged Man is a curious card because of the contradictions that are apparent. Despite the fact that the man is hanging by his foot, his face expresses deep entrancement and even a hint of a smile. In the Colman Smith design he has a nimbus round his head and the figure is hanging from wood that is obviously living as it is covered with leaves. In the Marseilles deck the branches are leafless. This card symbolises life in suspension rather than death, which may appear to be the first impression.

Divinatory Meaning

The presence of a Major Arcana card will dominate a reading and will carry more weight than Minor Arcana cards. The Hanged Man card is number twelve and therefore a three (1 + 2 = 3). Threes in a reading indicate a period of suspended activity before future success can be achieved. There is a focus on reflecting on what is happening here and now. The querent should think of ways in which he or she can make compromises in order to avoid failure. The Hanged Man represents wisdom, circumspection, discernment, trials, sacrifice, intuition, divination, prophecy and change. This card reveals that the querent is experiencing an awakening of his or her intuitive powers, and he or she will find this enriches his or her life.

Reversed Meaning

When the Hanged Man appears in the reversed position in a reading it represents selfishness, the crowd, lack of effort and lack of compromise. The querent may find it difficult to progress at this time as he or she is acting stubbornly and making no compromises. This behaviour could well result in the querent experiencing losses, perhaps losing friends.

Special Consideration
The Hanged Man serves as a reminder to the querent of the importance of intuition and psychic powers that defy scientific explanation.

Death, Morte

Pictorial Symbolism

The thirteenth card, traditionally going unnamed, shows a skeleton, with a scythe, seemingly reaping a harvest of human body parts which lie at his foot. Has the figure cut off his own foot? The Pamela Colman Smith design is a much more elaborate one. Death is represented by one of the apocalyptic visions. Behind the figure of Death lies the whole world of ascent in the spirit. The mysterious horseman moves slowly, bearing a black banner emblazoned with the mystic rose that signifies life. Between two pillars on the verge of the horizon the sun of immortality shines. The horseman carries no visible weapon but falling in front of him are a king, a child and a maiden, and a man of the church awaits his end with clasped hands.

Divinatory Meaning

The presence of a Major Arcana card will dominate a reading and will carry more weight than Minor Arcana cards. The Death card is number thirteen and therefore a four ($1 + 3 = 4$). Fours in a reading indicate the realisation of one's goals. There is a focus on endings and beginnings, good and bad. The Death card represents changes, endings, morality, corruption, rebirth and beginnings. The presence of the Death card indicates to the querent that a stage in his or her life is coming to an end but that from this ending new experiences will evolve. Once the ending is complete the querent will be able to progress to the future and let go of the past.

Reversed Meaning

When the Death card appears in the reversed position

in a reading it represents stagnation, inertia, lethargy and destruction. The querent may lack motivation at this time and be constantly looking for courses of action that require little effort. The querent should try to find enthusiasm for life or the destructive nature of this behaviour will take its toll.

Special Consideration

The Death card indicates to the querent that it is necessary to look at what is happening in his or her life and to question the amount of energy that he or she is putting into relationships that are not progressing. The querent needs to decide whether it is necessary to let go in order to save energy.

Temperance, Temperanza

XIV

Temperance

Pictorial Symbolism

A winged woman pours water from one chalice to another. This symbolises union, possibly of opposites. In the Colman Smith design there is a figure of a winged angel with the sign of the sun on its forehead. On its breast it has the square and triangle of the septenary (the number seven). The figure is pouring the essences of life from one chalice to another. The angel stands with one foot on the earth and with one foot in the water, which illustrates the nature of the essences of life. To the left of the figure there is a path leading to a range of mountains on the distant horizon. Above the mountain range is a great light – part of the secret of eternal life lies here.

Divinatory Meaning

The presence of a Major Arcana card will dominate a reading and will carry more weight than Minor Arcana cards. The Temperance card is the number fourteen and therefore a five $(1 + 4 = 5)$. Fives in a reading indicate a time of changes and of ups and downs. There is a focus on reassessing situations that seemed to be behind the querent but have re-emerged. The Temperance card represents moderation, frugality, management, accommodation and economy. The presence of the Temperance card in a reading indicates to the querent that it is necessary to live frugally and manage affairs carefully at this time.

Reversed Meaning

When the Temperance card is in the reversed position in a reading it represents conflicts, competing interests, divisions and hostilities. The querent may be feeling self-indulgent at this time, which could lead to those involved with the querent being angered by his or her selfish behaviour. The result of this situation could well be disputes and arguments. To avoid this the querent should act less selfishly and be more considerate of others.

Special Consideration

The Temperance card indicates to the querent that he or she is entering into a time of recuperation, both spiritually and physically. At this time it is important to keep distractions to a minimum in order to allow the process of healing to be completed.

The Devil, Le Diable

The Devil

Pictorial Symbolism

A winged devil who seems to have breasts as well as a penis, stands with hand aloft and sword in the air. He is accompanied by two sexless enslaved creatures. Slavery is an important symbol as this card represents that from which the querent wishes to escape. Again, a more elaborate design is followed for the Colman Smith/Waite deck. The card shows a figure, the Horned Goat of Mendes, with wings like those of a bat, standing on an altar. At the pit of his stomach there is the sign of Mercury. The right hand is upraised and extended, being the reverse of the benediction given by the Hierophant. In the figure's left hand there is a great flaming torch inverted towards the earth. A reversed pentagram is on the forehead. There is a ring in front of the altar from which two chains are carried to the necks of two figures, one male and one female. These are analogous with those on the fifth card, as if Adam and Eve after their fall from grace.

Divinatory Meaning

The presence of a Major Arcana card will dominate a reading and will carry more weight than Minor Arcana cards. The Devil card is number fifteen, therefore a six ($1 + 5 = 6$). When there are sixes in a reading it indicates adaptability and the need to make changes in times of difficulty. This card usually indicates that the querent is involved in a negative situation but that his or her ability to get out of it is low due to clouded judgment. It represents violence, force, failure, disaster, death and ominous events. When the querent draws the Devil card it signifies that the querent should reflect on the present situation and ask others for advice so that they can escape this period of stagnation and frustration that they are sufferign from. The querent should work towards solving difficulties cautiously and slowly.

Reversed Meaning

When the Devil card appears in the reversed position in a reading it represents weakness, pettiness and blindness. The querent may be experiencing a weakness of the spirit at this time and therefore be blind to faults, both his or her own and others. Such blindness and lack of perception may cause the querent harm, and he or she should try to find strength at this time.

Special Consideration

Although the Devil card has a sinister quality, it should not be feared. This card indicates to the querent that it is necessary to focus energies on positive thoughts and actions instead of draining oneself by wasting energy on negative aspects.

The Tower, La Torre, The House of God, La Maison Dieu

The House of God

Pictorial Symbolism

On the surface this card depicts ruin in all its aspects. The Tower is said to be derived from the Tower of Babel, which is written about in the Bible as well as other historical works. One version of events tells how the Tower of Babel contained all the knowledge of the world in a library. God destroyed this library to show that knowledge alone does not make a person great; a person needs humility and wisdom in order to make sense and good use of knowledge. This interpretation of the Tower then indicates that the Tower is symbolic of false hopes and ideas.

Divinatory Meaning

The presence of a Major Arcana card will dominate a reading and will carry more weight than Minor Arcana cards. The Tower card is a number seven card ($1 + 6 = 7$). When readings contain sevens, it indicates a time of solitude and asking questions of oneself. When the Tower card is drawn in a reading there is a focus on sudden and complete change, unexpected events and separations. When the querent draws the Tower card it is nearly always an indication of unwelcome change. The Tower card represents misery, distress, adversity, deception and ruin. The querent would be well advised to seek advice and help. It is important for the querent not to lose heart as it is possible to rebuild after changes. The other cards in the reading will indicate which area of the querent's life is subject to change and to what extent the querent will suffer.

Reversed Meaning

When the Tower card is drawn in the reversed position

in a reading it represents oppression, imprisonment, tyranny and ongoing depression. The querent may feel dominated by another or by a situation and will feel powerless to fight back at this time. The querent should concentrate on the future and on ways to redress the balance of power.

Special Meaning

The Tower card should be seen as an indication that the time has come to make a new start. The querent should have inner peace and be aware of the whole picture rather than be held back by dwelling on the negative changes.

The Star, L'Étoile, Stella

The Star

Pictorial Symbolism

The main feature on the card is a large radiant with eight rams surrounded by seven similar but smaller stars. In the foreground there is a figure of a naked woman. She has her left knee on the land while her right foot rests on the water. She has in her hand two vases from which she pours Water of Life – one into the sea and one onto the land. Behind the figure there is a bird resting in a shrub on a hill. The figure represents eternal youth and beauty. The Star card represents hope and the beauty of the natural world.

Divinatory Meaning

The presence of a Major Arcana card will dominate a reading and will carry more weight than Minor Arcana cards. The Star card is a number eight card (1 + 7 = 8), and eights in a reading are very positive and indicate positive changes. When the Star card is drawn in a reading, there is a focus on what may lie ahead in the future. The Star card indicates to the querent that recent difficulties will soon disappear and a new more positive future will begin. The Star card represents hope, bright prospects, new opportunities and just rewards. On drawing this card, the querent should feel a sense of relief and calm. The querent may well experience new independence and inner strength in the near future.

Reversed Meaning

When the Star card appears in the reversed position in a reading it represents loss, impotence and lack of success. The querent may experience temporary setbacks and may be easily taken in by a conman or be the victim of a theft.

Special Consideration

The Star shines a light of hope and promise on the querent. It is sometimes said that the Star card rewards a faith in oneself and in fate.

The Moon, La Luna

XVIII

The Moon

Pictorial Symbolism

In the centre of the picture there is the moon with sixteen main and sixteen secondary rays. In the foreground there are two dogs representing the fears of the natural mind in the presence of the unknown. The presence of the dogs and a creature from the sea have been interpreted as illuminations of our animal nature, with the sea creature representing the part of our nature that is lower than a savage beast. In the picture the creature is trying to attain manifestation by crawling out of stagnant looking water. But as a rule it will generally sink back. The moon directs a calm face on the unrest below.

Divinatory Meaning

The presence of a Major Arcana card will dominate a reading and will carry more weight than Minor Arcana cards. The Moon card is number eighteen and therefore a nine card ($1 + 8 = 9$). Nines in a reading indicate the completion of events. When the Moon card is drawn in a reading there is a focus on inner fears and uncertainties. The Moon card indicates that the querent would be wise to pay attention to intuitive feelings and inner voices. The querent should be wary, as at this time he or she is open to threats and dangers. The Moon card represents hidden enemies, danger, darkness, deception and errors.

Reversed Meaning

When the Moon card appears in the reversed position in a reading, it represents instability, inconsistency, silence and minor problems. The querent may be involved in a difficult situation at this time, which is adversely affecting his or her health and inner strength.

Special Consideration

The Moon card shows the querent that at some point it will be necessary for him or her to face up to the situation and accept it for what it is in order to make any changes. The Moon card should inspire the querent to be true to himself or herself.

The Sun, Le Soleil

The Sun

Pictorial Symbolism

The sun streams down on two figures. They are children, half naked and surrounded by a walled garden. They are touching each other signifying that they are partners facing the world together. In the foreground of the Colman Smith card is the figure of a naked child mounted on a white horse. The child represents simplicity and innocence in humanity. Behind the figure is a walled garden spilling forth life in all forms. The sun dominates the horizon, being the source of light and warmth for the earth below. Without the sun there would be no life on earth. The child figure is outside the walled garden and is making the transition from the known world of earth into the unknown world beyond.

Divinatory Meaning

The presence of a Major Arcana card will dominate a reading and will carry more weight than Minor Arcana cards. The Sun card is number nineteen and therefore a one card ($1 + 9 = 10$ and $1 + 0 = 1$). Ones in a reading indicate new beginnings and change. When the Sun card is drawn in a reading, there is a focus on relationships with others and on self-knowledge. The Sun card indicates that the querent is contented with his or her position in life and knows inner peace and that success and happiness will be ongoing. This is very positive card. The Sun card represents material happiness, contentment, accomplishment and successful unions. If the querent is contemplating marriage or commitment, this card indicates that it will be a successful union.

Reversed Meaning

When the Sun card appears in the reversed position in a reading it represents minor successes but the querent should be wary of over committing himself or herself and should exercise caution. The querent may feel pompous and vain at this time, which could result in a blurring of judgment and the querent may be persuaded to make rash decisions.

Special Consideration

The presence of this card in a reading indicates a very positive stage in the querent's life. The querent has achieved a new level of spiritual maturity and is now benefiting from this.

Judgement, Le Jugement, Angel, Angelo

XX

Judgement

Pictorial Symbolism

There is a figure of a great angel encompassed by clouds. The angel blows a trumpet which has a flag of a cross attached to it. Below the angel, the dead are rising from their tombs. The scene shows the awakening of awareness and spiritual enlightenment that are not possible to achieve in this life. It is a representation of eternal life.

Divinatory Meaning

The presence of a Major Arcana card will dominate a reading and will carry more weight than Minor Arcana cards. The Judgement card is number twenty and therefore a number two card $(2 + 0 = 2)$. Twos in a reading indicate a period of gestation, of warmth and anticipation of future successes. When the Judgement card is drawn in a reading, there is a focus on change and new developments. The Judgement card indicates to the querent that it is important to deal with matters that have been previously put aside in order to advance to new successes. The Judgement card often indicates that there will be significant changes in the querent's life – new relationships, a new career or a new home. The Judgement card represents change of position, renewal and spiritual development.

Reversed Meaning

When the Judgement card appears in the reversed position in a reading it represents weakness, delays, deliberation, indecision and regrets. The querent may be involved in a legal dispute, and the presence of this card suggests that the decision will go against the querent, and the querent may regret his or her previous behaviour.

Special Consideration

The Judgement card will highlight any injustices that exist in the querent's life. The querent should be inspired to work towards the future and accept that there may not be any signs of material success for a while.

The World, Le Monde

The World

Pictorial Symbolism

The World card represents the completed journey of the Fool. The Fool has found freedom and the struggles of life have been temporarily suspended. The figure of a naked woman on the card holds a wand, symbolising power on earth. These figures show the development of man. The figure has the attention of the four elements of the world – earth, fire, water and air – represented by the four figures outside her oval.

Divinatory Meaning

The presence of a Major Arcana card will dominate a reading and will carry more weight than Minor Arcana cards. The World is number twenty-one and therefore a three card (2 + 1 = 3). Threes in a reading suggest that there is more than one person involved and can also indicate that there will be a period of suspended activity before future success. When the World card is drawn in a reading, there is a focus on a significant change in the querent's life. This card could indicate that the querent may move overseas for a period. It shows that the querent has completed his or her inner journey and is now knowing inner peace at this stage in life. The World card indicates assured success, voyage, emigration and goals achieved.

Reversed Meaning

When the World card appears in the reversed position in a reading it represents inertia, stagnation and permanence. The querent may lack courage and conviction at this time. An opportunity may arise and the querent will have to act quickly and decisively. If he or she does not take advantage of this opportunity there may be regrets in the future.

Special Consideration

The querent should regard the presence of the World card as an inspiration to seize the day and attempt to fulfil his or her desires. If the querent is contemplating a significant change this card indicates that it will be successful.

The Minor Arcana

The Minor Arcana, or pip cards, of the Tarot de Marseilles have a divinatory meaning mostly based on numerology rather than pictorial symbolism. For this reason it may be easier for the novice to use the 22 cards of the Major Arcana for their readings.

Ace of
Wands

Divinatory Meaning

If the reading contains many Wands, it signifies that notions are taking place in the querent's mind. When an Ace is drawn in a reading, it is an indication of new beginnings as it is a number one card. The focus is on the querent achieving his or her potential and being open to new opportunities. The presence of this card in a reading indicates that the querent is feeling energised and ambitious. The querent will be inclined to make ambitious plans, but others may lack the same enthusiasm and vision. The Ace of Wands represents creation, invention, enterprise, birth, family, origin, virility and fortune. The querent may also feel spiritually awakened and enlightened.

Reversed Meaning

When the Ace of Wands appears in the reversed position in a reading it represents decadence, ruin, perdition, false start and blind optimism. It shows that the querent has a tendency to take things to the extreme. The querent may cause offence to others by being rude and tactless, the result of which could be disastrous for the querent.

Special Consideration

The Ace of Wands is a very powerful card that signifies awakening energies. The querent should be conscious of all new opportunities even from unsuspected sources. Keeping an open mind is very important.

Two of Wands

Divinatory Meaning

Twos in a reading indicate a period of gestation, of waiting and anticipation, and of great success in the future. If the reading contains many Wands, it signifies that notions are taking shape in the querent's mind. When the Two of Wands is drawn there is a focus on the querent's relationship to others. This card indicates a need for independence and solitude. The Two of Wands represents boldness, restricted freedom, dominance from another and separation. The querent may feel the need for a separation in order to feel in control of his or her destiny.

Reversed Meaning

When the Two of Wands appears in the reversed position it represents sadness, trouble, fear and loss. Although the querent may feel low at this point, change is imminent and hope should not be lost.

Special Consideration

The querent should assert his or her independence and not allow others to deny him or her this freedom. He or she should not allow him or her to be drawn into something against his or her will. Be strong or you may have regrets.

Three
of Wands

Divinatory Meaning

If the reading contains many Wands, it signifies that notions are taking place in the querent's mind. Threes in a reading suggest that more than one person is involved and can also suggest that there will be a period of suspended activity before future successes are realised. The focus is on cooperation and business opportunities. This indicates a time of moving forward and activity. The Three of Wands represents established strength, enterprise, effort, trade, commerce and discovery. The querent will feel pleased with how things are going but should remember those who helped to make it possible.

Reversed Meaning

When the Three of Wands appears in the reversed position in a reading it represents disappointments, toil and treachery. The querent will find others to be uncooperative and should be wary of mixed loyalties.

Special Consideration

The querent should be optimistic but should concentrate only on aspirations and goals that can be realised in order to avoid disappointments.

Four
of Wands

Divinatory Meaning

If the reading contains many Wands, it signifies that notions are taking place in the querent's mind. Fours in a reading indicate the realisation of one's goals. There is a focus on relationships. This is a positive card that indicates that relationships are going well or that problems will soon pass. The Four of Wands represents harmony, haven, romance, peace, concord and prosperity. This card indicates to the querent a quiet time spent with friends and family in a favourite place.

Reversed Meaning

When the Four of Wands appears in the reversed position in a reading its meaning does not alter and is therefore equally positive.

Special Consideration

The querent should enjoy this period when he or she will experience inner peace as well as harmony with others. This card indicates that a very positive time will be enjoyed by the querent.

Five
of Wands

Divinatory Meaning

If the reading contains many Wands, it signifies that notions are taking place in the querent's mind. Fives in a reading indicate a time of changes and of ups and downs. There is a focus on inner conflicts and a clash of personal ambitions. The presence of this card indicates the need for a struggle or confrontation in order to move on from a situation that has become stagnant. The Five of Wands represents strenuous competition, gain and courage. The querent needs inner strength and resolve in order to weather the storm, and this card in a reading shows that he or she has the strength that is required.

Reversed Meaning

When the Five of Wands appears in the reversed position it represents litigation, disputes, trickery, complications, contradictions and frustrations. The reversal of this card indicates more negative and bitter struggles that may result in the unpleasant sides to people's characters appearing.

Special consideration

It is important for the querent to be honest with himself or herself about what he or she wants or needs. Once the querent establishes his or her desire, he or she is in a position to fight to win.

Six
of Wands

Divinatory Meaning

If the reading contains many Wands, it signifies that notions are taking place in the querent's mind. Sixes in a reading indicate adaptability and the ability to change in times of difficulty. There is a focus on success and victory. This card indicates deserved victory after a period of struggle. The querent could well receive some great news that will enhance the victory. The Six of Wands represents triumph, victory, good news, high expectations, glory, hope and advancement. The querent should take the time to celebrate. He or she has faced some difficult times previously and is now in a position to relax and be happy.

Reversed Meaning

When the Six of Wands appears in the reversed position it represents apprehension, fear, treachery, disloyalty and vulnerability. The querent feels uneasy and needs to face up to his or her adversaries in order to clear the air.

Special Consideration

The querent would be well advised to offer friendship and conciliation to old adversaries rather than gloat about his or her success. The querent will be far happier within himself or herself once efforts have been made to repair friendships.

Seven
 of Wands

Divinatory Meaning

If the reading contains many Wands, it signifies that the querent's mind is full of ideas. Sevens in a reading represent a time of solitude and questioning oneself. The focus is on the courage of the querent. This card in a reading indicates that the querent has an already displayed courage by standing up to a problem that could easily have been ignored. The Seven of Wands represents valour, discussion, difficult negotiations, competition in business, and success over enemies. This card shows that the odds may be against the querent but that he or she should stand firm.

Reversed Meaning

When the Seven of Wands appears in the reversed position it represents, embarrassments, anxiety and confusion. The querent should be warned against indecision as it can lead to an adversary gaining the upper hand.

Special Consideration

The querent should not only concentrate on challenges externally but also within. In order to progress the querent should be prepared to make changes to himself or herself by challenging that which requires improvement.

Eight
of Wands

Divinatory Meaning

If the reading contains many Wands, it signifies that notions are taking place in the querent's mind. Eights in a reading are very positive and represent positive changes. There is a focus on fast-moving events and actions. If the querent is waiting for a reply to a letter, he or she will not have long to wait. The response could contain the promise of new love. The Eight of Wands represents swiftness, great haste, great hope, Cupid's arrow of love, and assured felicity. If a situation has been stagnant for some time, the querent may be surprised by a rapid progression towards a conclusion.

Reversed Meaning

When the Eight of Wands appears in the reversed position in a reading it represents jealously, internal dispute, stingings of conscience, quarrels, domestic disputes and lack of harmony. This situation could be brought about by an impetuous letter of hasty and ill-thought-out comment.

Special Meaning

The querent is aware of his or her desires and should take the initiative to realise them. This is a positive time and a time to make changes.

Nine of Wands

Divinatory Meaning

If the reading contains many Wands, it signifies that notions are taking place in the querent's mind. Nines in a reading indicate the completion of events. There is a focus on strength in opposition. It indicates that there could be a suspension of events, with the querent having the advantage at the present time. The presence of this card suggests that there has been conflict previously and there could be more ahead. The Nine of Wands represents boldness, readiness, strength, suspension, delay and adjournment. This card could signify that the querent is recovering from an illness.

Reversed Meaning

When the Nine of Wands appears in the reversed position it represents obstacles, adversity, calamity and a lack of initiative.

Special Meaning

The querent should not lose faith. He or she will need to be strong at this time in order to deal with future complications. The outlook in the long term is more positive.

Ten of Wands

Divinatory Meaning

If the reading contains many Wands, it signifies that notions are taking place in the querent's mind. (1 + 0 = 1). Ones in a reading indicate new beginnings and change. The focus is on success but success that has little reward. The presence of this card indicates that the querent is not at peace with himself or herself and is acting in a selfish manner. The querent may well receive material rewards at this time but spiritually this is a poor time. The Ten of Wands represents material gain, oppression, disguise, selfishness and excessive demands. If the querent is involved in a lawsuit he or she will almost certainly face defeat.

Reversed Meaning

When the Ten of Wands appears in the reversed position in a reading it represents contrarieties, difficulties, intrigues and deceit. The querent should be aware of others conspiring against him or her unexpectedly.

Special Consideration

To regain inner peace the querent should try to be more generous to others, both emotionally and materially. Material success is far more rewarding if the gains are shared.

*Page
of Wands*

Page of Wands

Divinatory Meaning

If the reading contains many Wands, it signifies that notions are taking place in the querent's mind. The Page of Wands represents the astrological sign of Sagittarius. The focus is on receiving news. The querent should expect to receive good news that will cheer him or her. It could also indicate that a young man will be a faithful friend during a difficult time. The Page of Wands in a reading represents faithfulness, a postman, a lover, an envoy, a messenger, consistency and stability. This card can also indicate that family problems will come to an end.

Reversed Meaning

When the Page of Wands appears in the reversed position in a reading it represents bad news, indecision, instability and reluctance. A young person could be the source of bad news.

Special Consideration

A close friend could help to enlighten the querent, and the querent could see things from a new perspective.

Knight
of Wands

Knight of Wands

Divinatory Meaning

If the reading contains many Wands, it signifies that notions are taking place in the querent's mind. The presence of a knight in a reading indicates that a situation will soon change. The focus is on the need to make important decisions. The querent could be making a journey abroad. Other changes that may be happening in the querent's life could be a new residence, a new relationship or a new business connection. The Knight of Wands represents departure, absence, flight, emigration and change of residence. The querent may find himself or herself receptive to prophetic visions at this time.

Reversed Meaning

When the Knight of Wands appears in the reversed position in a reading it represents rupture, division, interruption, discord and conflict. This state of affairs could be brought about by a person making offensive remarks.

Special Consideration

The realisation of the querent's goals is imminent and the querent should continue to have faith.

Queen
of Wands

Queen of Wands

Divinatory Meaning

If the reading contains many Wands, it signifies that notions are taking place in the querent's mind. The Queen of Wands is associated with the astrological sign Leo. The focus is on family matters and relationships. This card indicates that the querent will encounter a friendly and loving woman. This woman may bring the querent success in business. The Queen of Wands represents a woman – friendly, chaste, loving, honourable – success in business and material gain.

Reversed Meaning

When the Queen of Wands appears in the reversed position in a reading it represents jealously, deceit, a turned friend, false pride, snobbery and stupidity.

Special Consideration

After a lull the querent's spiritual development will be renewed. It is important to seek advice from others during this time.

King
of Wands

King of Wands

Divinatory Meaning

If the reading contains many Wands, it signifies that notions are taking place in the querent's mind. The King of Wands is linked with the astrological sign of Aries. The presence of this card in a reading indicates that there is a focus on the querent's ambitions. This card indicates that the querent will have a favourable encounter with an assertive male who will support the querent during a difficult time. As a result of this encounter the querent may benefit financially. The King of Wands in a reading represents honesty, unexpected inheritance, friendship, nobility and loyalty.

Reversed Meaning

When the King of Wands appears in the reversed position in a reading it represents unpredictability, bigotry, contradictory behaviour on another's part and severity. The querent should be wary of characters whose integrity is doubtful, and he or she should be prepared to remain calm in a possible crisis.

Special Consideration

Although the querent will gain much from the support of the male that he or she will meet, it is important to remember one's own strengths and abilities. This is a time during which the querent is feeling confident and should use this confidence to inspire others whose situations are less favourable.

Ace
of Cups

Divinatory Meaning

The presence of many Cups in a reading indicates a time during which the querent's actions will revolve around emotions. An Ace in a reading indicates new beginnings and is a number one. There is a focus on awakenings of new thoughts concerning inner desires. The presence of the Ace of Wands in a reading suggests that the querent is enjoying a time of pleasure and contentment. The querent will feel spiritually enlightened and at peace both with himself or herself but also with the world at large. The Ace of Cups represents joy, contentment, nourishment, abundance, fertility and spiritual fulfilment.

Reversed Meaning

When the Ace of Cups appears in the reversed position in a reading it represents instability, revolution and mutation. This could indicate that the querent is feeling anxious, which could result in instability, but the Ace of Wands is a generally favourable card and this should reassure the querent.

Special Consideration

As this is such a positive time for the querent it is a good time to explore new experiences. This card suggests that the querent will be successful in any pursuit.

Two
of Cups

Divinatory Meaning

The presence of many Cups in a reading indicates a time during which the querent's actions will revolve around emotions. Twos in a reading indicate a period of gestation, of waiting and anticipation of great success in the future. There is a focus on relationships and matters of the heart. The presence of this card in a reading indicates the simple unity of two people in love. If the querent is forming a new relationship, this card's presence suggests that it will be extremely rewarding and successful. If the querent is in an ongoing relationship there will be renewed passion and communication. The Two of Cups in a reading represents love, passion, friendship, affinity, union, concord, sympathy and harmony.

Reversed Meaning

When the Two of Cups appears in the reversed position in a reading it represents almost the exact opposite – disharmony, separation, divorce and unsuccessful relationships. Partnerships could falter because too much energy is being put into them, creating an intense and suffocating relationship.

Special Consideration

The querent may find love with someone he or she had not previously thought of in a romantic way – it is important to keep an open mind and to be open to possibilities.

Three
of Cups

Divinatory Meaning

The presence of many Cups in a reading indicates a time during which the querent's actions will revolve around emotions. Threes in a reading suggest that more than one person is involved and can also suggest that there could be a period of suspended activity before future successes are realised. There is a focus on acceptance both of one-self and of others. The presence of the Three of Cups in a reading indicates that any problems that have arisen in the past will be resolved and the querent will be free to celebrate. The Three of Cups represents perfection, mer-riment, victory, fulfilment, solace and healing. The querent may receive some good news at this time.

Reversed Meaning

When the Three of Cups appears in the reversed position in a reading it represents excessive physical enjoyment on the part of the querent.

Special Consideration

If the querent has experienced difficult relations with another in the past, this would be a good time to clear the air and try to establish a friendship. The querent should accept the positive traits and strengths of others as well as his or her own.

Four
of Cups

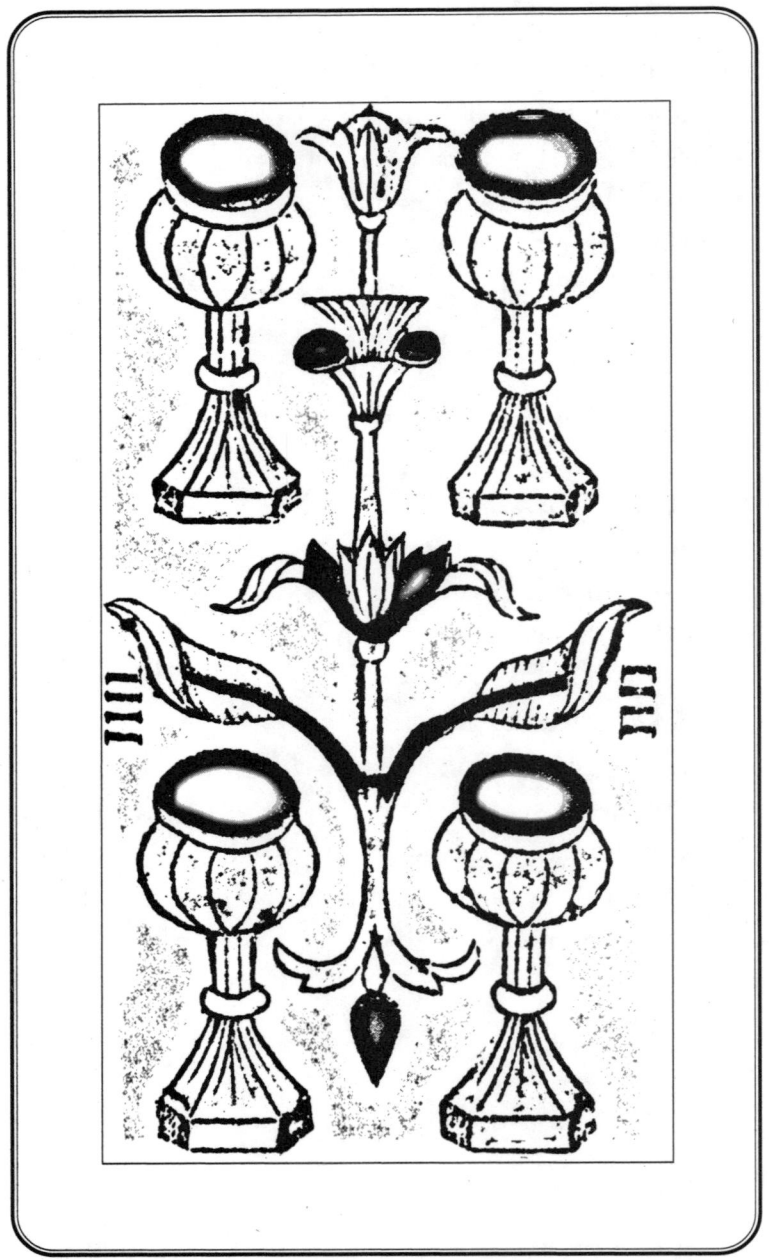

Divinatory Meaning

The presence of many Cups in a reading indicates a time during which the querent's actions will revolve around emotions. Fours in a reading indicate the realisation of one's goals. There is a focus on blended pleasure and weariness. The querent may be feeling anxious about an offer that has been made, and there may be doubts about the repercussions of accepting it. The querent should assess what has already been gained and compare this to what could be gained from the offer. The querent will need to contemplate the benefits and risks – it would be better to err on the side of caution. The Four of Cups represents weariness, compromise, anxiety, mistrust and hesitation.

Reversed Meaning

When the Four of Cups appears in the reversed position in a reading it represents novelty, new relations, new instructions and possibilities. This clearly indicates that the querent will experience new beginnings.

Special Consideration

The querent should not give in to anxieties and difficulties in the present. The future will hold new opportunities and successes.

Five
of Cups

Divinatory Meaning

The presence of many Cups in a reading indicates a time during which the querent's actions will revolve around emotions. Fives in a reading indicate a time of changes and of ups and downs. There is a focus on loss. The querent may experience a feeling of bitterness that could create real problems in a relationship. This card is frequently associated with marital difficulties and divorce. The querent may receive an inheritance, but this will bring little pleasure. The Five of Cups in a reading represents bitterness, frustration, inheritance, regret and depression.

Reversed Meaning

When the Five of Cups appears in the reversed position in a reading it represents news, alliances, affinity, ancestry, return and hope. The querent may hear news that an old friend will soon return.

Special Consideration

In time the bitterness and emptiness that the querent is feeling will pass, and feelings of contentment and happiness will return. The querent should consider his or her reasons for these negative feelings and try to establish a positive goal or desire.

Six
of Cups

Divinatory Meaning

The presence of many Cups in a reading indicates a time during which the querent's actions will revolve around emotions. Sixes in a reading indicate adaptability and the ability to change during difficult times. There is a focus on new environments and nostalgia. The changes that may occur in the querent's life may not have manifested themselves yet as this card indicates that the changes are in very early stages. The querent may meet up with old friends and enjoy reminiscing about the past together. The Six of Cups represents childhood, happiness, enjoyment, new environments, new employment and memories of the past.

Reversed Meaning

When the Six of Cups appears in the reversed position in a reading it represents the future, renewal and living in the past. This card could indicate that the querent is finding it difficult to face the future and feels lacking in emotional strength.

Special Consideration

The querent will feel peaceful at this time and will enjoy life's simple pleasures. The querent may even experiment with arts and crafts and discover hidden talents.

Seven
of Cups

Divinatory Meaning

The presence of many Cups in a reading indicates a time during which the querent's actions will revolve around emotions. Sevens in a reading indicate a time of solitude and asking questions of oneself. There is a focus on deception. The querent will be faced with an offer that may seem too good to be true. It would be prudent to delay making any firm decisions until it is easier to see the truth – at this time the querent will find the truth hard to find. The Seven of Cups represents fairy favours, images of reflection, sentiment, imagination and little achievement. The querent may find his or her senses clouded by emotional ties and sentimental feelings.

Reversed Meaning

When the Seven of Cups appears in the reversed position in a reading it represents desire, will, determination and success. The querent may be filled with strong emotions that help to achieve success. It is important to remember that success is not everything and can lead to spiritual poverty.

Special Consideration

The querent should not be disheartened by the delay in activities. It would be wise to use the time to reflect on the positive aspects that already exist in his or her life.

*Eight
of Cups*

Divinatory Meaning

The presence of many Cups in a reading indicates a time during which the querent's actions will revolve around emotions. Eights in a reading are generally very positive and represent positive changes. There is a focus on the completion of events. The querent may have been caught up in events that have been complicated and costly. The presence of this card indicates that the querent has decided to move on and leave the past behind. He or she will cut all ties with the events and will not even give them a thought once they are in the past. The Eight of Cups in a reading represents the decline of a matter, slight consequences, withdrawal and abandonment.

Reversed Meaning

When the Eight of Cups appears in the reversed position in a reading it represents great joy, happiness, material success and feasting.

Special Consideration

Once the querent has made the decision to move on, his or her attention will turn to seeking happiness and fulfilment. The querent will be filled with optimism, which is a good start when seeking happiness.

Nine
of Cups

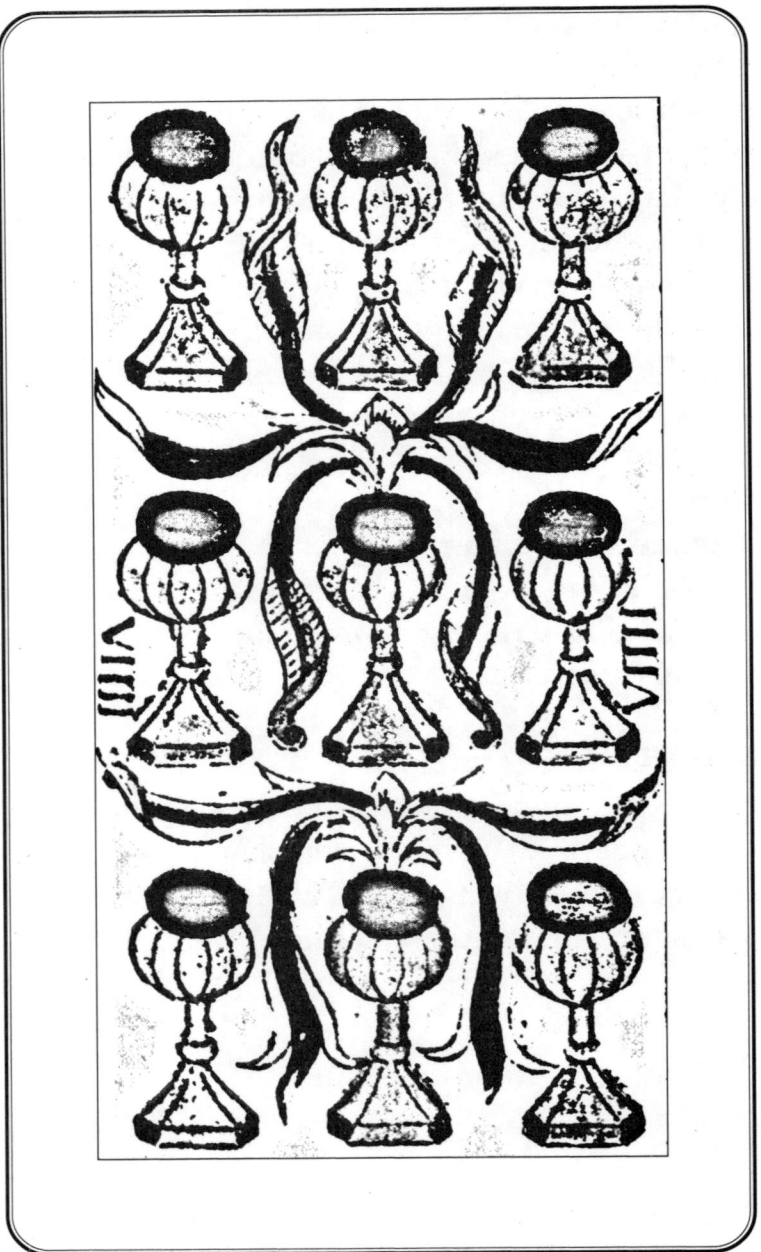

Divinatory Meaning

The presence of many Cups in a reading indicates a time during which the querent's actions will revolve around emotions. Nines in a reading indicate the completion of events. There is a focus on harmony and balance. This is an extremely positive card to draw in a reading as it indicates that the querent is overwhelmed by a feeling of complete happiness on all levels. It could be that an enterprise undertaken has come to a successful conclusion. The Nine of Cups in a reading represents concord, contentment, victory, success, harmony, satisfaction and advantage.

Reversed Meaning

When the Nine of Cups appears in the reversed position in a reading it represents mistakes, imperfections, vanity and lack of humility. This card indicates that the querent may have been selfish and careless in victory, which led to mistakes being made.

Special Consideration

The querent should make the most of this very positive time and use his or her good fortune to help others whose fortunes have not been so good. Generosity and kindness bring their own rewards.

Ten
of Cups

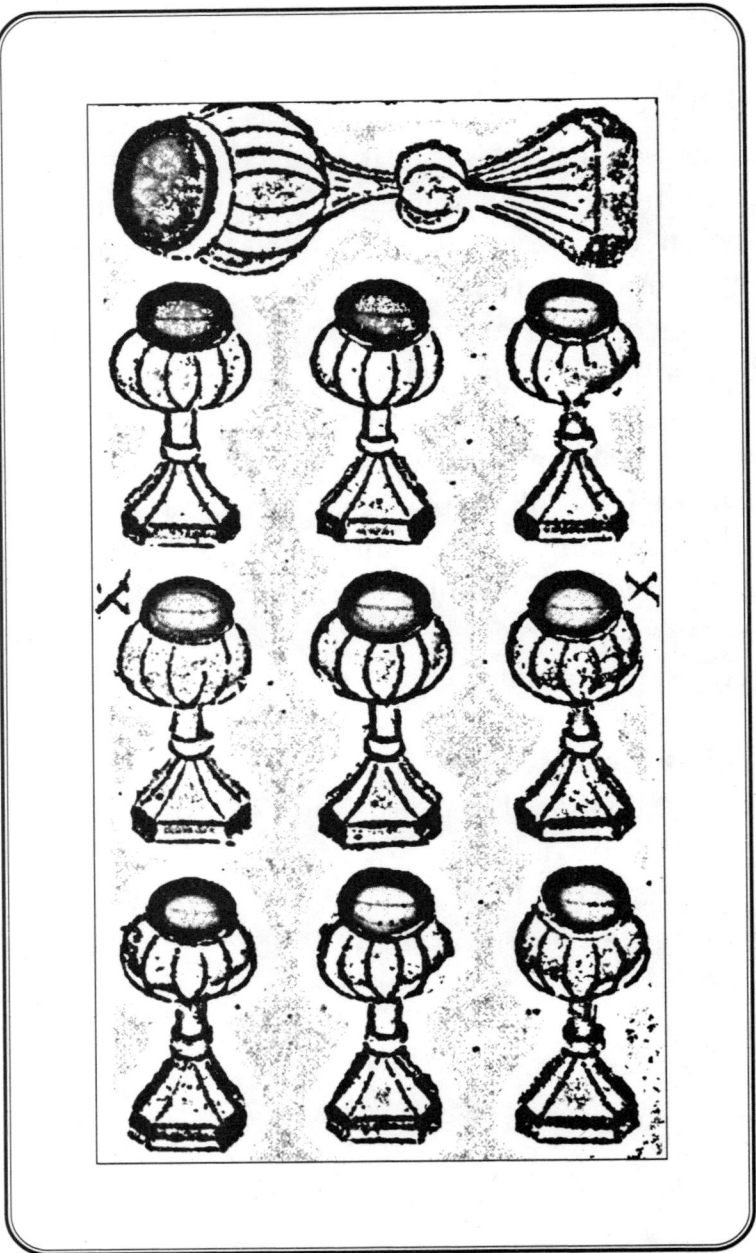

Divinatory Meaning

The presence of many Cups in a reading indicates a time during which the querent's actions will revolve around emotions. Ones in a reading $(1 + 0 = 1)$ indicate new beginnings and change. There is a focus on relationships. The querent will find that at this time relationships are harmonious and pleasurable. The querent may also feel a desire to be more involved in his or her home life and the community. The Ten of Cups in a reading represents contentment, repose of the entire heart, perfection, human love, friendship, family and home.

Reversed Meaning

When the Ten of Cups appears in the reversed position in a reading it represents conflict, broken relationships, a lack of harmony and false promises. The querent should not give in to the negative qualities of this card and should try to be strong in the face of adversity.

Special Consideration

This is a very strong card to be present in a reading and its meaning will not be detracted from by other cards. The querent should use this positive time to benefit those he or she loves and cares for.

Page
of Cups

Page of Cups

Divinatory Meaning

The presence of many Cups in a reading indicates a time during which the querent's actions will revolve around emotions. The Page of Cups is associated with the astrological sign of Pisces. There is a focus on news and business. The querent may hear some significant news, perhaps about the expansion of a business or a proposal of marriage. This news may come from someone who is gentle and artistic but who can surprisingly show courage and valour in times of need. The Page of Cups in a reading represents news, message, application, reflection, meditation and business issues.

Reversed Meaning

When the Page of Cups appears in the reversed position in a reading it represents seduction, deception, artifice, distractions and attachment. The querent may find himself or herself being seduced by fanciful ideas and false promises.

Special Consideration

The querent should be wary of accepting proposals too readily. He or she should assess what the heart truly desires and decide if he or she is ready for a significant change. There will be further opportunities in the future and if the time is not right now the querent should let this opportunity pass by.

Knight of Cups

Divinatory Meaning

The presence of many Cups in a reading indicates a time during which the querent's actions will revolve around emotions. The presence of a knight in a reading indicates that a stagnant situation will soon change. There is a focus on imagination and inspiration. The querent may be approached by a messenger bringing news that will have a powerful effect on his or her imagination. The querent may be overcome by strong emotions of passion and excitement. The Knight of Cups in a reading represents an invitation, arrival, approach, a messenger, propositions, enticements and imagination.

Reversed Meaning

When the Knight of Cups appears in the reversed position in a reading it represents trickery, artifice, subtlety, swindling, duplicity and fraud. The querent may be targeted by a character with much charisma.

Special Consideration

The querent should beware the intentions of an dishonest character who may be about to do the querent harm. The querent should take care that his or her emotions do not overrule common sense.

Queen
of Cups

Queen of Cups

Divinatory Meaning

The presence of many Cups in a reading indicates a time during which the querent's actions will revolve around emotions. The Queen of Cups is associated with the astrological sign of Scorpio. There is a focus on development. The querent will enjoy the company of others at this time. The presence of this card indicates that the querent's relationships are strong and pleasurable. The Queen of Cups in a reading represents goodness, honesty, devotion, success, happiness, pleasure, wisdom, virtue and intelligence. The querent may well encounter a wise and loving woman who will be influential.

Reversed Meaning

When the Queen of Cups appears in the reversed position in a reading it represents deception, lack of trust, dishonour and falseness. The querent should exercise caution if he or she meets a woman who is apparently distinguished and popular as this woman could be untrustworthy and not all that she seems.

Special Consideration

This is a positive time for the querent and an excellent opportunity to strengthen relationships. At this time the querent will be feeling full of wisdom and should share his or her knowledge and experiences with others.

King
of Cups

King of Cups

Divinatory Meaning

The presence of many Cups in a reading indicates a time during which the querent's actions will revolve around emotions. The King of Cups is associated with the astrological sign of Cancer. There is a focus on business matters. The querent may well encounter a man who promises to be helpful in a business matter, and this could prove to be true. However, the querent should stay involved in the matter as the man may lose interest and enthusiasm towards the end, at which point the querent will need to step in. The King of Cups in a reading represents business, responsibility, creative intelligence, law and divinity.

Reversed Meaning

When the King of Cups appears in the reversed position in a reading it represents dishonesty, a double-dealing man, roguery, exaction, injustice, vice, scandal and considerable loss. If this card appears in a reading the querent would be well advised not to become involved in any new ventures with an unknown man.

Special Consideration

The querent may encounter a man of religious beliefs who may arouse the querent's interest in spiritual development.

Ace
of Swords

Divinatory Meaning

If a reading contains many Swords, it indicates a time of great activity in the querent's life. When an ace is drawn in a reading it is an indication of new beginnings as it is a number one card. There is a focus on critical and potentially volatile situations. The querent may well find himself or herself in the position of having to take action or make a decision under stressful circumstances. It is important for the querent to attempt to keep emotions balanced in order to make the correct decision. The Ace of Swords in a reading represents triumph, the excessive degree in everything, conquest and forceful emotions.

Reversed Meaning

When the Ace of Swords appears in the reversed position in a reading it represents disaster, destruction, excessive use of negative forces and hate triumphing over love. This card indicates that the balance of strong emotions has tipped strongly towards the negative, which is creating disastrous situations. The querent should try to stop the downward spiral and try to regain a balance of emotions.

Special Consideration

Once the querent has achieved a balance of emotions, he or she will go on to triumph and will enjoy success.

Two
of Swords

Divinatory Meaning

If a reading contains many Swords, it indicates a time of great activity in the querent's life. Twos in a reading indicate a period of gestation, of waiting and anticipation of great success in the future. There is a focus on negotiations. If the querent has been involved in a dispute with a friend or acquaintance, the presence of this card indicates that an amicable solution will be reached, with both parties feeling positive and glad that the dispute is over. The Two of Swords in a reading represents courage, friendship, concord, affection, communication, compromise and harmony.

Reversed Meaning

When the Two of Swords appears in the reversed position in a reading it represents duplicity, falsehood, disloyalty and release. The querent should be wary of another who seeks a compromise but is unwilling to make concessions.

Special Consideration

The key to achieving a satisfactory compromise is open and honest communication. The querent should not let previous bitterness influence the communication. Once a compromise has been reached the querent should feel a sense of achievement at having been open-minded and considerate of others.

Three
of Swords

Divinatory Meaning

If a reading contains many Swords, it indicates a time of great activity in the querent's life. Threes in a reading suggest that more than one person is involved and also suggest that there will be a period of suspended activity before future successes are realised. There is a focus on separations and loss. Unfortunately this card indicates an unhappy time in the querent's life. The querent may well be experiencing difficulties in a relationship that could lead to separation. The cause of these difficulties is likely to be jealousy or interference by another party. The Three of Swords in a reading represents removal, absence, delay, division, rupture, depression and separation.

Reversed Meaning

When the Three of Swords appears in the reversed position in a reading it represents mental alienation, error, loss, distraction, disorder and confusion. The querent may find that he or she is becoming obsessed with negative experiences that are happening in the present and are denying previous happier times. The querent should step back from the situation and try to be more objective.

Special Consideration

The querent should try not to be too depressed by the negative events taking place. They will not last forever and once this difficult time is over he or she will feel a sense of release and wellbeing.

Four
of Swords

Divinatory Meaning

If a reading contains many Swords, it indicates a time of great activity in the querent's life. Fours in a reading indicate the realisation of one's goals. There is a focus on retreat and contemplation. The querent has previously been involved in complicated and highly charged situations involving many people. The querent now feels the need for solitude and a chance to meditate and be at peace with himself or herself. The Four of Swords in a reading represents vigilance, retreat, solitude, repose and exile.

Reversed Meaning

When the Four of Swords appears in the reversed position in a reading it represents isolation, loneliness, detachment and seclusion. The presence of this card in a reading indicates that the querent has been in retreat for too long or at the wrong time, and has become cut off and may have missed out on opportunities as a result. The querent should make attempts to re-integrate and socialise.

Special Consideration

The querent will feel truly at peace during this time of solitude and may find spiritual enrichment through meditation and reading. However, the querent should be wary of cutting ties with friends and should not isolate himself or herself.

Five
of Swords

Divinatory Meaning

If a reading contains many Swords, it indicates a time of great activity in the querent's life. Fives in a reading indicate a time of changes and of ups and downs. There is a focus on bitterness and frustration. The querent may have been involved in a conflict that has brought to light an unpleasant and devious side of his or her character. Such is the nature of this type of conflict that no party will win or triumph as the parties involved will sink to any level to try to win. The result will be unhappiness and grief for both parties. The Five of Swords in a reading represents degradation, destruction, dishonour, infamy, loss and devastation.

Reversed Meaning

When the Five of Swords appears in the reversed position in a reading it represents uncertainty, weakness, humiliation and mortification. The querent will be antagonised by a rival, and gossip and rumours will spread round the querent's friends. The querent should be strong at this time and should not feel pity for the rival as it will be interpreted as weakness.

Special Consideration

The querent should be aware of the negative aspects of his or her character that are surfacing and should try to redress the balance by acting positively and not giving in to the negative desires. Using positive affirmations in meditation may help the querent to feel more positive.

Six
of Swords

Divinatory Meaning

If a reading contains many Swords, it indicates a time of great activity in the querent's life. Sixes in a reading indicate adaptability and the ability to change in times of difficulty. There is a focus on obstacles overcome. The querent may have been struggling with difficult situations recently, but this card indicates that the querent has managed to achieve a balance and to create order in his or her life. The querent may well feel in need of a break or holiday, and this card indicates that he or she will travel, possibly over water. The Six of Swords in a reading represents journeys, routes, success, resolution of difficulties, peace and calm.

Reversed Meaning

When the Six of Swords appears in the reversed position in a reading it represents regrets, disappointments, disillusionment, travel and journey. The querent may well decide to go away for a break in order to get over disappointments. The querent will benefit from the break and will return with a lighter heart.

Special Consideration

The querent should recognise the new skills and strengths that were developed during the time of difficulties that he or she experienced. These skills and strengths will have made the querent a stronger person, and in future times of difficulty he or she will be able to draw on these new strengths.

Seven
of Swords

Divinatory Meaning

If a reading contains many Swords, it indicates a time of great activity in the querent's life. Sevens in a reading represent a time of solitude and of asking questions of oneself. There is a focus on adjustments and ill-conceived plans. The querent may be involved in a scheme that is moderately successful. Another person may approach the querent with ideas of how to improve the venture. The querent should be wary of fanciful promises and should look carefully at the situation before making adjustments. The querent needs to remain concentrated at this time and should keep distractions to a minimum. The Seven of Swords in a reading represents design, attempts, wishes, hopes, confidence, quarrelling, a plan that may fail, and annoyance.

Reversed Meaning

When the Seven of Swords appears in the reversed position in a reading it represents confusion, bad timing, loss of concentration and defeat. This card indicates that during a struggle the querent chose to relax at the wrong time, and this resulted in the other party taking advantage, leaving the querent confused.

Special Consideration

If the plan does not work out the querent should not look to place the blame on others but should look to himself or herself for reasons for the failure. This card indicates that the most likely cause of failure is hasty actions and lack of concentration.

*Eight
of Swords*

Divinatory Meaning

If a reading contains many Swords, it indicates a time of great activity in the querent's life. Eights in a reading are generally positive and represent positive changes. There is a focus on imprisonment. The querent may be feeling trapped by a situation in his or her life, and is unable to express his or her feelings. The querent may become involved in several unsuccessful ventures in an attempt to gain freedom. The Eight of Swords in a reading represents crisis, conflict, censure and entrapment.

Reversed Meaning

When the Eight of Swords appears in the reversed position in a reading it represents disquiet, difficulty, opposition, treachery and hopelessness. The querent may be feeling weighed down by the confines of his or her situation and be unable to see any reason to be hopeful. The querent should be strong and try to fight for his or her liberty.

Special Consideration

Although the querent is feeling trapped by his or her situation, the mind is free and full of activity. The querent should use this time to reflect on how the situation came about and how he or she will act once it is over. Once the querent is free of his or her prison, he or she will feel a new sense of determination and strength.

Nine
of Swords

Divinatory Meaning

If a reading contains many Swords, it indicates a time of great activity in the querent's life. Nines in a reading indicate the completion of events. There is a focus on suffering and anxiety. This card is often associated with miscarriages and accidents, and the unbearable mental torment that follows such events. The querent may well be feeling very low at this time and may find it difficult to keep the strength needed to carry on. The Nine of Swords in a reading represents failure, miscarriage, delay, deception, disappointment, despair and death. This is an introspective time for the querent, and others who wish to help will find they get little response.

Reversed Meaning

When the Nine of Swords appears in the reversed position in a reading it represents doubt, suspicion, imprisonment, fear, guilt and shame. The querent may be depressed because he or she is feeling guilty about something that has happened. This depression could affect the querent's physical wellbeing, and he or she should try to seek help for the depression before he or she becomes very ill.

Special Consideration

As the querent is feeling very low at this time, he or she has little energy so the best way to cope is to let fate run its course without fighting it. Eventually this depression will lift and happiness will re-enter the querent's life.

Ten
of Swords

Divinatory Meaning

If a reading contains many Swords, it indicates a time of great activity in the querent's life. Ones in a reading $(1 + 0 = 1)$ indicate new beginnings and changes. There is a focus on failure and destruction. Despite the violent scene depicted on the card, this card does not necessarily represent a violent attack. It does suggest, however, that the querent's enemies have weapons that could be used to cause the querent harm. The presence of this card indicates that the destructive situation that the querent is involved in has reached a climax, and in the near future the querent will be able to think more clearly. The Ten of Swords in a reading represents pain, affliction, tears, sadness and desolation.

Reversed Meaning

When the Ten of Swords appears in the reversed position in a reading it represents advantage, profit, success, favour, power and authority. However, these will all be short-term benefits and will lack permanence.

Special Consideration

The querent should look carefully at the other cards to get an impression of which area of his or her life will be effected by this card. It is important for the querent to stay strong as this card represents the end of a negative situation and the beginning of change. The querent will experience a clarity of thought as a result of the recent traumas.

Page
of Swords

Page of Swords

Divinatory Meaning

If a reading contains many Swords, it indicates a time of great activity in the querent's life. The Page of Swords is associated with the astrological sign of Taurus. There is a focus on perception. The presence of the card indicates that the querent is involved in a secretive situation that requires skills of observation, devotion and subtlety. The Page of Swords in a reading represents authority, overseeing, secret service, vigilance, spying, agility and examination.

Reversed Meaning

When the Page of Swords appears in the reversed position in a reading it represents underhanded deeds, deceit, deviousness and callousness. The card in this position suggests that the secretive person's actions have become malicious. As a result bad feelings will surface and may result in a violent confrontation.

Special Consideration

The querent should be aware that secretiveness can lead to confusion and lack of trust. The querent should not leave close friends in the dark as they may wrongly interpret the situation and reach their own conclusions.

Knight
of Swords

Knight of Swords

Divinatory Meaning

If a reading contains many Swords, it indicates a time of great activity in the querent's life. The presence of a knight in a reading indicates that a stagnant situation will soon change. There is a focus on reckless actions. The querent may find himself or herself involved with a person who acts impulsively and whose thoughts are erratic. This person could either be an enemy of the querent or a loyal friend whose intention is to act in the querent's favour. The Knight of Swords in a reading represents skill, bravery, capacity, defence, address, wrath, war, destruction, opposition, resistance and ruin.

Reversed Meaning

When the Knight of Swords appears in the reversed position in a reading it represents imprudence, incapacity, extravagance and indiscretion. This suggests that actions are poorly thought out and that the querent has become too indulgent. It is necessary to step back from the situation and to think objectively in order to regain balance.

Special Consideration

The querent should pay careful consideration to the other cards in the reading as they hold the key as to which area of the querent's life will be affected. The querent should be wary of indulging in impulsive and erratic actions and should try to create balance by acting in a very stable manner.

Queen
of Swords

Queen of Swords

Divinatory Meaning

If a reading contains many Swords, it indicates a time of great activity in the querent's life. The Queen of Swords is associated with the astrological sign of Virgo. There is a focus on sadness but also perception. The Queen of Swords in a reading represents widowhood, female sadness, embarrassment, absence, sterility, mourning, privation, separation and intelligence. The querent may be involved with a woman who has experienced sorrow and has become dispassionate but quick-witted as a result. This woman can act quickly and severely.

Reversed Meaning

When the Queen of Swords appears in the reversed position it represents malice, bigotry, artifice, prudery and deceit. This card indicates that a woman, possibly the querent, has become embittered as a result of a sorrowful experience. This woman has a sharp tongue and can cause distress to others by making stinging comments.

Special Consideration

The querent should attempt to help the sorrowful woman come to terms with her misery before it turns to bitterness. The querent should highlight the positives that still exist in life and the potential joys that the future holds. It is important, however, to respect and acknowledge the pain and sorrow that the woman has experienced.

King
of Swords

King of Swords

Divinatory Meaning

If a reading contains many Swords, it indicates a time of great activity in the querent's life. The King of Swords is associated with the astrological sign of Libra. There is a focus on decisive actions. The King of Swords in a reading represents power, command, authority, militant intelligence, law and enforcement. This card indicates that the querent is, or is involved with, someone who is detached and determined in thought and action.

Reversed Meaning

When the King of Swords appears in the reversed position in a reading it represents cruelty, perversity, barbarity and evil intent. This card indicates that the querent is, or is involved with, a man who is tyrannical in his behaviour, a man who has become completely detached from human suffering and enjoys imposing his will. Although this man may appear calm and confident, his inner feelings are of great unhappiness.

Special Consideration

The querent should endeavour to ensure that the man does not become extreme in his detachment and cold-heartedness. The querent should highlight the consequences for others of actions that may benefit the man.

Ace of
Coins

Divinatory Meaning

If a reading contains many Coins, it signifies that the querent will feel that situations are taking form. When an ace is drawn in a reading it is an indication of a new beginning as it is a number one card. There is a focus on the realisation of goals. The querent may have been working towards a goal for some time, and the presence of this card suggests that the hard work has paid off. The rewards may be seen in a business venture or personal relationships. It may even signify the birth of a child. The Ace of Coins in a reading represents perfect contentment, ecstasy, gold, intelligence and joy.

Reversed Meaning

When the Ace of Coins appears in the reversed position in a reading it represents the evil side of wealth, preoccupation with material assets, prosperity and comfortable material conditions. The querent may have become spiritually impoverished as a result of material self-indulgence.

Special Consideration

This is a very positive time for the querent. However, the querent should be wary of being carried away by the luxuries of material wealth. It is always important to remember that there are others who lack such riches.

Two of
Coins

Divinatory Meaning

If a reading contains many Coins, it signifies that the querent will feel that situations are taking form. Twos in a reading indicate a period of gestation, of waiting and anticipation of great success in the future. There is a focus on the need for balance. This card in a reading suggests that situations in the querent's life could develop either positively or negatively, so the querent needs to juggle his or her affairs to keep the balance. There is the possibility that the querent may travel at this time. The Two of Coins in a reading represents gaiety, recreation, news, obstacles, agitation, trouble and embroilment.

Reversed Meaning

When the two of Coins appears in the reversed position in a reading it represents enforced gaiety, simulated enjoyment, a lack of willpower and disharmony. The querent's mind is preoccupied with a previous event. It is necessary for the querent to resolve this situation before he or she will feel truly joyful.

Special Consideration

If the querent is able to keep his or her affairs balanced, this will be a very positive time, and there will be a great many rewards. The querent will feel in control and euphoric.

Three of Coins

Divinatory Meaning

If a reading contains many Coins, it signifies that the querent will feel that situations are taking form. Threes in a reading suggest that more than one person is involved and can also suggest that there will be a period of suspended activity before future successes are realised. There is a focus on the recognition of skills and hard work. The querent may find that employers or potential employers have taken note of his or her abilities and quality of work. The querent may be called on to work on a project that will benefit from his or her skills. The Three of Coins in a reading represents trade, skilled labour, renown, glory and recognition.

Reversed Meaning

When the Three of Coins appears in the reversed position in a reading it represents mediocrity, pettiness, weakness, lack of skill and inefficiency. The querent may have made grand plans regarding a work venture but later lost interest and enthusiasm, resulting in sloppy work. It may be best to cut one's losses if renewed motivation can not be found.

Special Consideration

The querent will get a great amount of personal satisfaction from the success of the venture and from recognition from others. The spiritual rewards will be great though the material gain may be less than expected.

Four of
Coins

Divinatory Meaning

If a reading contains many Coins, it signifies that the querent will feel that situations are taking form. Fours in a reading indicate the realisation of one's goals. There is a focus on material wealth. The querent may receive a large sum of money that will ensure his or her financial security. This money may be an inheritance or a golden handshake from an employer. The Four of Coins in a reading represents gifts, legacies, inheritance and wealth.

Reversed Meaning

When the Four of Coins appears in the reversed position in a reading it represents suspense, obstacles, delay, opposition and loss. Others have become jealous of the querent's wealth and are plotting to create obstacles.

Special Consideration

This card indicates that the querent will enjoy a rewarding time financially at this time. In order to gain this material wealth, however, it seems that the querent may experience a loss. Inheritance may be gained through the death of a relative or close friend, and a golden handshake would mean the end of a time of employment. Such losses may leave the querent feeling alone and lost, and financial security is sometimes cold comfort.

Five of Coins

Divinatory Meaning

If a reading contains many Coins, it signifies that the querent will feel that situations are taking form. Fives in a reading indicate a time of changes and of ups and downs. There is a focus on financial or personal difficulties. The querent may experience problems at work that can cause concerns regarding financial security. Problems in a relationship may arise from arguments about money or because infidelity is suspected. The Five of Coins in a reading represents poverty, emotional problems, loneliness, troubled thoughts and financial insecurity.

Reversed Meaning

When the Five of Coins appears in the reversed position in a reading it represents disorder, chaos, ruin, discord and loss. The querent may feel that circumstances are outside his or her control, and the querent's health may begin to suffer as a result. The querent should look for ways to salvage what can be saved and then cut his or her losses and start anew.

Special Consideration

The querent should examine his or her situation closely and decide if a solution is likely to present itself in the near future. If not, the best course of action may well be to bow out of the situation in the early stages rather than become involved in a draining struggle. Once definite action has been taken the querent will be free to mourn and grieve and then begin to heal and feel better.

Six of
Coins

Divinatory Meaning

If a reading contains many Coins, it signifies that the querent will feel that situations are taking form. Sixes in a reading indicate adaptability and the ability to make changes in times of difficulty. There is a focus on accomplishments and rewards. The querent may have been involved in a business venture that has proved to be a wise investment as financial rewards will be great. The querent will have achieved success through hard work and the success is deserved. The querent will be considerate of others, especially those who helped along the way, and will become known for his or her generosity. The Six of Coins in a reading represents presents, gifts, gratification, prosperity and attention.

Reversed Meaning

When the Six of Coins appears in the reversed position in a reading it represents envy, jealousy, desire, illusion and selfishness. The querent may be jealous of another's wealth and may live more extravagantly than his or her means allow.

Special Consideration

The querent may well find himself or herself in a very influential and powerful position, which will be demanding but also rewarding. The querent will also feel rewards from being able to be generous and charitable.

Seven of
Coins

Divinatory Meaning

If a reading contains many Coins, it signifies that the querent will feel that situations are taking form. Sevens in a reading indicate a time of solitude and asking questions of oneself. There is a focus on limited successes. The querent may be involved in a venture that has little financial reward but serves to help a friend. The querent will be satisfied once the enterprise is concluded as a debt will have been repaid and a job will have been done well. The Seven of Coins in a reading represents business, limited success, hard work and favours returned.

Reversed Meaning

When the Seven of Coins appears in the reversed position in a reading it represents anxiety, impatience, disappointments and concerns regarding money. A friend may approach the querent for a financial loan. The querent may have doubts about the friend's intentions or ability to repay the loan. The querent should not give the loan if lack of repayment would cause him or her financial difficulties.

Special Consideration

The querent may have resigned himself or herself to the fact that the project in which he or she is involved will be non-profitable, but it could be that a lack of vision is limiting the success. It is possible that with enthusiasm and hard work the venture could be more profitable than expected.

Eight of Coins

Divinatory Meaning

If a reading contains many Coins, it signifies that the querent will feel that situations are taking form. Eights in a reading are generally very positive and represent positive changes. There is a focus on the building of foundations for future success. The querent will be justified in having high hopes for the future as present situations and ventures are going well and the outlook is good. The querent will have worked hard to create this state of affairs, and continued hard work will be required. The Eight of Coins in a reading represents work, employment, commission, craftsmanship, skill, business and a bright future.

Reversed Meaning

When the Eight of Coins appears in the reversed position in a reading it represents vanity, exaction, a lack of ambition, avarice and greed. The querent may desire financial rewards but lacks the skill and ambition at this time to achieve it. The querent should be wary of seeking dishonest means of finding financial success as it could lead to spiritual impoverishment if others suffer as a result.

Special Consideration

The querent should not lose interest or involvement in other areas of his or her life and should be wary of becoming obsessed with the venture. Friends and those close to the querent may start to feel unneeded and seek fulfilment elsewhere if they are neglected.

Nine of
Coins

Divinatory Meaning

If a reading contains many Coins, it signifies that the querent will feel that situations are taking form. Nines in a reading indicate the completion of events. There is a focus on positive rewards. The querent may have been working on a venture alone. During this time the querent may have had to be self-sufficient and rely on inner strengths. This card suggests that the hard work will be paid off and will be recognised and rewarded. If the querent has recently heard of an inheritance it could well turn out to be of greater value than first thought. The Nine of Coins in a reading represents prudence, safety, success, accomplishment, discernment and certitude.

Reversed Meaning

When the Nine of Coins appears in the reversed position in a reading it represents roguery, deception, bad faith, danger and threats. The querent may be involved in the theft of a sum of money or the loan of money used for illegal gains.

Special Consideration

The querent will receive financial rewards, and these will bring pleasure. However, for the querent the real pleasure will come from knowing that he or she alone was responsible for the success, and the querent will be filled with a sense of self-worth.

Ten of
Coins

Divinatory Meaning

If a reading contains many Coins, it signifies that the querent will feel that situations are taking form. Ones in a reading $(1 + 0 = 1)$ indicate new beginnings and change. There is a focus on family matters. The querent will find that his or her home is the most powerful influence in his or her life at this time. It could be that another member of the querent's family is having a difficult time financially and the querent is in a position to help out. The Ten of Coins in a reading represents gain, riches, family matters, home and distribution of wealth.

Reversed Meaning

When the Ten of Coins appears in the reversed position in a reading it represents chance, fatality, loss and robbery. The querent may experience a temporary setback. Losses experienced at this time will be expected or minor.

Special Consideration

The querent now has the opportunity to repay his or her family for all its support and love. The querent will be able to show his or her gratitude by sharing his or her wealth and rewards.

Page of Coins

Page of Coins

Divinatory Meaning

If a reading contains many Coins, it signifies that the querent will feel that situations are taking form. The Page of Coins is associated with the astrological sign of Capricorn. There is a focus on study. If the querent has recently been studying for an examination the presence of this card in a reading suggests that the result will be favourable. This card indicates that the querent will receive some form of good news at this time. The Page of Coins in a reading represents application, study, scholarship, reflection, news and messages.

Reversed Meaning

When the Page of Coins appears in the reversed position in a reading it represents dissipation, concern, disappointment and rebellion. This could indicate that a young person in the querent's life has rejected study and caused disappointment.

Special Consideration

The querent will be rewarded for a period of study that required self-discipline and determination. The querent will feel proud of his or her efforts and will feel greater confidence in his or her abilities.

Knight of
Coins

Knight of Coins

Divinatory Meaning

If a reading contains many Coins, it signifies that the querent will feel that situations are taking form. The presence of a knight in a reading suggests that a stagnant situation will soon change. There is a focus on a hard-working character. The querent may be, or be involved with, a solid and trustworthy character who is keeping a venture going by doing hard work that is not always recognised or rewarded. The Knight of Coins in a reading represents patience, hard work, interest, responsibility and methodical work.

Reversed Meaning

When the Knight of Coins appears in the reversed position in a reading it represents inertia, idleness, stagnation, discouragement and carelessness. The querent or another may have an idea for a venture, but those approached for cooperation lack enthusiasm and motivation.

Special Consideration

The querent may benefit from the work and service of a solid man. The querent should appreciate his help and reward him justly. The character who is helping is likely to have a temper that is slow but once roused hard to cope with. The querent should be aware of this.

Queen of Coins

Queen of Coins

Divinatory Meaning

If a reading contains many Coins, it signifies that the querent will feel that situations are taking form. The Queen of Coins is associated with the astrological sign of Aquarius. There is a focus on ambitions and aspirations. The querent may encounter a sensible woman who will prove to be helpful in a business matter. The woman will be intuitive about other people and will be able to identify their strengths and weaknesses. The Queen of Coins in a reading represents opulence, generosity, security, liberty and magnificence.

Reversed Meaning

When the Queen of Coins appears in the reversed position in a reading it represents evil, suspicion, suspense, fear and mistrust. The querent may encounter a woman who causes problems in the querent's social circle and arouses feelings of mistrust.

Special Consideration

Situations are going well for the querent at this time and will continue to do so. The querent should be thankful to the woman who is offering help in business matters but should not lose confidence in himself or herself and become reliant on her perception.

*King of
Coins*

King of Coins

Divinatory Meaning

If a reading contains many Coins, it signifies that the querent will feel that situations are taking form. The King of Coins is associated with the astrological sign of Gemini. There is a focus on financial success. The querent may encounter a man who is able to offer guidance and assistance in a financial matter. This man will be wise in business matters but lacking in social graces and an appreciation of the arts. The King of Coins in a reading represents valour, intelligence, business aptitude and mathematical gifts.

Reversed Meaning

When the King of Coins appears in the reversed position in a reading it represents vice, weakness, ugliness, perversity, corruption and peril. The querent may encounter a bitter man who seeks to cause others harm and misfortune.

Special Consideration

The querent may well have a great deal of respect for the man who shows such intelligence regarding business matters but should not try to be like him. The querent should recognise that the man lacks spiritual riches and leads quite a lonely life.

Glossary

cartomancy   the art of telling fortunes by using cards.

court cards   the Kings, Queens, Knights and Pages of the suits of the Minor Arcana.

Coins   one of the suits of the Minor Arcana also sometimes known as Pentacles, depending on the deck.

Cups   one of the suits of the Minor Arcana.

deck   a pile of cards.

divination   the act of predicting events.

divinator   one who foretells events.

divinatory   the interpretation of individual cards.

meaning   the possible implications for the querent.

Major Arcana   the first twenty-two cards in a Tarot pack.

Minor Arcana   the remaining fifty-six cards divided into four suits.

New Age   a movement or philosophy concerned with spiritual harmony and ecology.

occult   the supernatural.

pack   a set of cards.

Pentacles   one of the suits of the Minor Arcana
                    which is also known as Coins.

**pictorial   interpretations of Tarot cards based
symbolism**   on the picture alone.

Querent   the person who seeks advice from the
                    Tarot cards.

reading   the interpretation of a spread of
                    Tarot cards.

significator   the card chosen to represent the
                    querent or situation in question.

**special   further advice as to the best course
consideration**   of action relating to individual cards.

spread   the arrangement of Tarot cards in
                    patterns that allow divination.

suit   one of the four sets in the Minor
                    Arcana of a Tarot pack.

Swords   one of the suits of the Minor Arcana.

Wands   one of the suits of the Minor Arcana.

Appendices:

Character Reading by the Cards

Sincerity and Sympathy

The qualities required to read the cards successfully are a good memory, a fine sense of the meaning of words, absolute sincerity and a wholehearted sympathy with the person whose cards you are reading (here called the subject).

A sense of the meaning of words is valuable in order to relate the interpretation of the cards properly. The good card-reader will not say '*very* lucky' when he or she only means 'lucky'; nor should a reader say '*extremely* dangerous' when 'dangerous' is sufficiently emphatic.

The card-reader must be *sincere*. He or she must empty his or her mind of all thoughts, except those required to explain each card correctly and to interpret its message with regard to the cards around it, which will confirm or modify its meaning. Sincerity insists that the card-reader must be entirely *selfless*.

The card-reader must be sympathetic. He or she must never claim that a reading is bad except as a warning to the subject, it may frighten the subject unnecessarily. A reader should choose their words carefully, e.g.: 'avoid that person'; 'do not keep this engagement'; 'do not let yourself get entangled with these matters or with those people,' 'take care in that situation.'

Sincerity and sympathy are not incompatible. Cards can only tell what is known, although neither the subject nor the card-reader may actually be aware of it. Things are already sure to happen in the future because of something that has been said, done, or that has happened in the past; or because of something that is now happening though we may have no knowledge of it.

Note that the truth and usefulness of divination by cards depends on the intelligence, sincerity, and sympathy of the subject also. The subject who gives concentration, honesty, and love equal to that of the earnest card-reader, will be guided and helped.

The Picture Cards

Kings are men of weight – older men.
Queens are women and girls.
Jacks are young, unmarried men.

The Suits

Spades stand for very dark people; Clubs for dark or brown-eyed people and Hearts for all who are neither fair nor dark – those with dark hair and blue or grey eyes, the chestnut-coloured people and the warm blondes, with eyes that range from the darkest blue to coldest agate grey. These are the largest class, the people called 'between colours'. Diamonds stand for the very fair, the 'lint-white' people, for the red-haired, and for those who are quite silvery white.

The subject must identify each Picture Card, after choosing 'herself' or 'himself' according to sex and colouring.

But these Picture Cards (or Court Cards) have additional meanings in certain combinations and under certain conditions.

It is only necessary, for the present, to realise that Spades represent trouble, anxieties, sorrows and changes that cannot be helped or hindered. Clubs mean success which has been earned or deserved. Hearts mean love, affection, company, socialising, and Diamonds stand for money, business and financial affairs in general.

Diamonds and Spades are 'chancy' suits; they stand for *fated* things, whether good or evil. Hearts represent things that can be altered by goodwill and sympathy. Clubs correspond to matters that, with some effort, may well be changed for the better.

The Cards Reversed

Some cards have a right way up and a reversed way. However, this is only the case with the Sevens and some odd numbers according to the way the centre 'pip' stands, and with all the cards when they are turned over *if* the design on the back has a 'right way up' and a 'reversed' way. Many designs are so ornate and intricately patterned that no difference can be seen, whichever way the cards come into your hand.

It is, therefore, wise to put 'R' on the top left hand corner of each card after turning the pack the wrong way up, if you can. (It depends on the design on the back; otherwise you devise your own 'reversed' way, excepting the Sevens.)

The meaning of each card is considerably modified if and when it is, 'reversed.' In some cases it is altered entirely.

Some card-readers do not recognise different meanings in the cards when they are 'reversed.' But the seer who wants to tell of subtle shades of meanings will do so from the first.

The Meaning of the Cards

Diamonds

Ace: A ring; paper money. *Rev:* A letter about money or containing money.

King: A fair or white-haired man. *Rev:* A treacherous man.

Queen: A fair girl or woman with white hair. *Rev:* A coquette, or flirt.

Jack: A fair youth. *Rev:* A selfish relative, man or woman.

Ten: Money. *Rev:* Journey concerning money.

Nine: Sharp instruments; anger. *Rev:* Operation. With Spades; loss by death.

Eight: Short journey; roadway; walk. *Rev:* Small money; a gain that will not last.

Seven: Child or pet. *Rev:* Disappointing money.

Six: Hope. *Rev:* Trouble with subordinates.

Five: Gold, riches. *Rev:* The law; proceedings.

Four: Society. *Rev:* Happiness.

Three: Trade. *Rev:* Separation.

Two: Fortune, sum of money. *Rev:* Surprise.

Hearts

Ace: The House; between King and Queen, a love letter. *Rev:* Change of residence.

King: A man 'between colours'. *Rev:* A fickle, inconstant man.

Queen: A woman 'between colours'. *Rev:* A vengeful woman.

Jack: A lover or one beloved. *Rev:* The best-beloved of consultant.

Ten: Great affection; happiness; corrects bad c a r d s. *Rev:* Change; birth.

Nine: Success; desires fulfilled; the *wish card*. *Rev:* Love.

Eight: Love and marriage; happy spending. *Rev:* Jealousy of men.

Seven: Inconstancy; small success. *Rev:* Jealousy of women.

Six: The past. *Rev:* The future.

Five: Marriage. *Rev:* Arrival.

Four: A messenger. *Rev:* Discontent.

Three: Success; near Spades, insecure; near Diamonds, with money; near Hearts, with love; near Clubs, with ambition. *Rev:* Opposition to plans.

Two: Love. *Rev:* Opposition to love.

Spades

Ace: Business; high building. *Rev:* Death; annoyance.

King: Very dark elderly man or a man handling important affairs. *Rev:* An enemy.

Queen: A dark lady; a widow. *Rev:* Plots and scandal. With her Jack, a dangerous woman.

Jack: A very dark young man. *Rev:* Night; shadow; medical matters.

Ten: Distance; across water; voyages. *Rev:* Sickness; trouble. With Eight of Hearts; bereavement.

Nine: Failure; loss; undoing. *Rev:* Death (corrected by good cards around it).

Eight: Night; illness. *Rev:* Deceit; plots. *Rev:* Between King and Queen, a separation.

Seven: Determination; change. *Rev:* Accident; upset. With Diamonds, most disappointing to present hopes.

Six: A voyage. *Rev:* A surprise.

Five: Mourning. *Rev:* A loss.

Four: Solitude. *Rev:* A proposal.

Three: A quarrel. *Rev:* Confusion.

Two: A friend. *Rev:* An enemy, once a friend.

Clubs

Ace: Letters; papers; good documents. *Rev:* Delayed letters; unpleasant news.

King: A brown-eyed man; a good friend. *Rev:* Worried or perplexed man.

Queen: A brown-eyed woman. *Rev:* A disappointed woman; sad.

Jack: A dark-eyed young man. *Rev:* The thoughts of the consultant.

Ten: A journey. *Rev:* Going across water.

Nine: A will or a legacy. *Rev:* A troubled journey; delays.

Eight: Affection of a 'club' man; good friend; ally. *Rev:* Papers; documents.

Seven: Victory. *Rev:* Financial worry; delayed success or achievement.

Six: Presents. Gifts. *Rev:* Ambition.

Five: A lover. *Rev:* Flirtation.

Four: Pleasure. *Rev:* Delays.

Three: Economy (keep your money!). *Rev:* Position; honour.

Two: Children. *Rev:* Letters.

Certain combinations may now be learned with these

meanings or they may be left until later on, when the student has mastered simple card-reading. However, the brief meanings given above must be mastered, before any 'reading' is attempted.

Certain Combinations

A Card 'with' one or two other cards, means that both or all three cards come out in the 'set-out' by either of the methods explained on pages 222–231.

The King of Hearts with the Nine of Hearts: A happy love.

The King of Hearts with the Ten of Hearts: Sincere love.

The Jack of Hearts with the Ten of Hearts: An ardent sweet-heart.

The Jack of Hearts with the Nine of Hearts: An engagement.

The Eight of Hearts between Court Cards: Helpful friends.

Ten of Hearts with the Ace of Spades: A birth.

The Ace of Diamonds with the Eight of Hearts: An engage-ment ring.

The Two Black Tens: A long voyage.

King of Clubs with Ten of Hearts: True love of friends.

Jack of Diamonds with Ten of Spades: Trouble and unrest.

Ace of Diamonds with Ten of Hearts: A wedding.

Court Card with Seven of Spades: Treachery of a friend.

Diamond Court Card with Nine of Clubs: A rival in love.

Jack of Spades with Nine of Diamonds: A physician.

Jack of Spades with Nine of Clubs: A lawyer.

Ace of Spades with Nine of Hearts: Fulfilled longings (of the senses).

Ace of Spades with Nine of Clubs: A theatre. A place of public amusement.

The Ace of Spades touching a Queen with the Eight of Spades near: illicit meetings.

Duplicates of the Same Card

Kings
Four Kings: Honours; dignities. *Rev:* Litigation.
Three Kings: Successful undertakings. *Rev:* New projects.
Two Kings: Friends in business. *Rev:* New projects.

Queens
Four Queens: Quarrels; scandal. *Rev:* Frivolity.
Three Queens: Society; convention. *Rev:* Scandal; gossip.
Two Queens: Friendly consultations. *Rev:* Gossip.

Jacks
Four Jacks: Treachery. *Rev:* A law court.
Three Jacks: Disputes; affronts. *Rev:* Indifference.
Two Jacks: A bill; a demand. *Rev:* False friends; treachery.

Tens
Four Tens: Success. *Rev:* An unpleasant surprise.
Three Tens: A happy future. *Rev:* Loss.
Two Tens: A lucky surprise. *Rev:* Excesses.

Nines
Four Nines: Robbery; imposition. *Rev:* Avarice; extreme greed.
Three Nines: Delay to projects. *Rev:* Greed of gain.
Two Nines: (Red) – Riches: (Black) – Disappointment. *Rev:* Loss.

Eights
Four Eights: Success. *Rev:* Disappointment; failure.
Three Eights: Thoughts of marriage. *Rev:* Amusement; frivolity; flirtations.

Two Eights:	Uncertain plans. *Rev:* An undertaking, commitment.

Sevens
Four Sevens:	Children. *Rev:* Intrigues.
Three Sevens:	Upset; disturbance. *Rev:* Domestic worries.
Two Sevens:	A proposal. *Rev:* Worries.

Note that satisfactory card-reading can be accomplished by some methods without using the smaller cards. The Sixes, Fives, Fours, Threes, and Twos mostly stand for ideas. Their use belongs to more difficult divination by cards.

Sixes
Four Sixes:	Ambition. *Rev:* Wisdom.
Three Sixes:	Generosity. *Rev:* Wealth.
Two Sixes:	Gain. *Rev:* Joy.

Fives
Four Fives:	Caution. *Rev:* Caution against unfaithful allies.
Three Fives:	Power. *Rev:* Wealth.
Two Fives:	Anxiety. *Rev:* Speed.

Fours
Four Fours:	Pleasure. *Rev:* Cleverness.
Three Fours:	Catastrophe. *Rev:* Suspicion.
Two Fours:	Extravagance. *Rev:* Speculation.

Threes
Four Threes:	Strategy. *Rev:* Disappointment.
Three Threes:	Deception. *Rev:* Success
Two Threes:	Victory. *Rev:* Loss; obstacles; success delayed.

Twos

Four Twos:	News. *Rev:* Indifference.
Three Twos:	Alarm. *Rev:* Treachery.
Two Twos:	A small wish. *Rev:* Self-control.

The Cut

You may cut the cards on every occasion, before beginning to comb out the cards that are to form the 'fortune' proper, by dealing them according to either of the following methods:

To cut – shuffle the cards well and put them into three lots, face upwards. Red cards are 'bright' cards, and are better than black cards. Two reds out of three cards are better than the other way about, that is, two black and one red.

But remember that Clubs are never bad. Although the Spades are not bad either, generally, they are not a cheerful suit.

Read the meanings of the Cards you have cut, reminding the subject (or yourself if you are telling your own fortune) that what is told by the cut may be in the distant future, and that *it may be avoided* if it is not good. The cut *is* true, yet it is not *sure* to come true! It has significance as a warning or a promise. But if the same cards reappear in the 'set-out' or 'fortune,' then their early fulfilment is emphasised.

Reading the Cards: First Method

You may now begin to cut the cards for yourself, that is, to tell your own fortune; for this will give you proficiency in handling, in reading, and in 'telling'. The first method makes use of all the cards in the pack.

Choose as 'yourself' a Queen if you are a woman, a King if a married man, a Jack if a single man. Choose the suit according to your complexion.

Shuffle the 52 cards well, and, if you are using a new pack, turn some of them about a few times, to get the 'reverse' meanings, if these want to come out.

Then deal the cards out one by one, saying as you turn each one up on the heap before you: 'King, Queen, Jack, Ten, Nine, Eight, Seven, Six, Five, Four, Three, Two, One, Heart'. (We give the Hearts an extra chance in each of the thirteen chances, because Hearts are always good, and human nature craves good news).

If a King of any suit comes out as you say 'King', put it out above the heap and begin again – 'King, Queen,' etc. If a Queen comes out when you say 'Queen,' a Two when you say 'two,' an Ace when you say 'one' or a Heart, when you say 'Heart', always put the agreeing card out, and always begin again, saying the list in order of value. You would have to begin again when you say 'Heart' whether an agreeing card came out or not, for *Heart* is the last of the line.

When you have gone through the pack, take up the cards that have been thrown out again. However, do not begin with 'King' unless the last card was in agreement with your call and was put above in the 'fortune'. If your last card thrown in the heap was a Six, begin with 'five' when you commence to deal for the second time.

Repeat the deal a third time. That is, comb out the 'fortune' proper by three dealings of the cards that have not agreed with your calling of the List, the discarded cards.

The disadvantage of this first method is that you may

get very few cards out. In that case, things are probably going very uneventfully with you. Tell yourself 'Happy is the nation that has no History!'

Great or important events are not imminent, either, if you have quite a lot of cards of the smaller values, that is the 'under sevens'. Dealings with people are rare, if Picture Cards are absent or are few in the 'set-out'.

A lot of Picture Cards means company, or that you are going to meet people, even if festivity is not implied. But you may expect small worries if the small cards are mostly dark ones, especially if Spades predominate.

Spades are (roughly) anxieties, if not actual troubles.

Hearts are love, company, visiting, the home and pleasure.

Diamonds represent money and business matters.

Clubs, though black, are good and stand for success, power and achievement.

Spades and Diamonds are 'chancy' suits. You cannot help or alter or avoid the things for which they stand; and a lot of Diamonds, although they represent money, do not exactly mean money earned or money which you can increase.

Hearts and Clubs are happier, more pleasant suits.

If, however, 'you' (the card that stands for 'yourself') come out, you can control the indications in the 'set-out'; you *can* improve matters if there are a lot of Spades in your 'fortunes'; and you *can* increase the good promise of the Hearts or Clubs that have come out.

The Nine of Hearts is the best card in the pack; the Nine of Spades the worst. When this last is 'out' by this first method and 'you' are not out, you must just 'sit tight'; do not attempt to do things – if you do, your efforts will come to nothing.

Remind yourself that the Cards may tell a brighter tale in a day or two.

Now read the Cards you have combed out – they may be three or they may be thirty-three – by this dealing of the whole pack three times. Keep in mind the simple meanings you have learned.

Reading the Cards: Second Method

In this second method you only use the cards above the Sixes, that is the four Aces, Kings, Queens, Jacks, Tens, Nines, Eights, and Sevens.

Shuffle the 32 cards and deal, counting each card you throw out thus, 'One, two, three, four, five, six'. Put the seventh card in a line above the heap of discarded cards. Count six again and throw them out, add the seventh card to the first above. Repeat until you have only four cards in your hand.

Count these and throw them out, pick up the discards again and go on, saying 'five, six, seven'; place this third one out above; count six and put the seven always in the line above the discarded cards. On this occasion your last card will be the seventh and should be placed in the line above. Then pick up the pile of discards and continue counting and placing the seventh card in the line above until you are left with three cards. Count these out and pick up the discards counting out 'four, five, six'; the seventh card will be placed above and the rest of the pack set aside leaving you with twelve cards for the fortune reading.

Notice whether it is the black or red cards that predominate. Read the combinations and then 'read the fortune'.

Do not read these twelve cards one by one, as in the first method. Count to the seventh and then count to the fourteenth, which will be the third from the first card at the left hand. Count on from seven from this, and add its meaning to the seven further on, going back always to the beginning, or the first card at your left. Do this, getting six (double-card) meanings, as you end on the twelfth or last card in the 'set-out'.

If you want to get more from the reading, you may now couple the cards, reading the first and the twelfth, the second and the eleventh, the third and the tenth, and so on until the last pair, the sixth and the seventh, have been read in conjunction.

When you become more skilful, you may shuffle the twenty smaller cards and add one of them to each of your 'couples'. But remember that these twelve cards are the 'Fortune' proper, and that the small cards are only used to obtain further light on what the six 'pairs' tell you.

Note that this second method gives you more of a story to tell, owing to the linking up of the meanings of two cards every time.

You can get to be a *reliable* card-reader, with constant practice of these two easy methods.

Advanced Card Reading

You may stick to these two methods and extract all that is to be got out of the cards, although there are very many more systems. Some of these are very intricate indeed.

The secret of success, provided you are intelligent, sincere and sympathetic, is to know the meanings of the cards in the very fullest sense.

Here are the more involved shades of meanings. However, first note that each of the 52 cards can be allotted to each of the 52 weeks in the year.

You can get your 'Luck of the Week', by one single cut of your cards. It is not necessarily 'Bad Luck' if you do *not* cut 'the Card of the Week'. It means a deservedly successful week if you cut 'yourself', especially if you have Clubs with you, for then the success is *earned*.

But a really bright and shining success is indicated if you cut 'the Card of the Week', as listed below.

It will prove advantageous to learn these meanings, and all the deeper possibilities, as given in this advanced style of card-reading. You will find yourself gaining a tremendous amount of knowledge, if you use the methods you have already learned *after* you have memorised the meanings of the cards of each week in the year.

Note that the weeks of the year are not read always from Sunday to Saturday in this connection; but always according to what day New Year's Day falls on. Thus 'the Week' may be from Tuesday to Monday if New Year's Day was on Tuesday; from Friday to Thursday, if 1 January was a Friday and so on.

The Cards of the Weeks

'I,' is for the first week in January and is represented by the Seven of Hearts. The rest follow in sequence as in this list:

I	The Seven of Hearts
II	The King of Clubs
III	The Eight of Diamonds
IV	The Ace of Hearts
V	The Five of Clubs
VI	The Three of Spades
VII	The Nine of Hearts
VIII	The Two of Clubs
IX	The Queen of Diamonds
X	The Jack of Spades
XI	The Ten of Clubs
XII	The Four of Diamonds
XIII	The Two Of Spades
XIV	The Nine of Diamonds
XV	The King of Hearts
XVI	The Eight of Spades
XVII	The Six of Clubs
XVIII	The Seven of Diamonds
XIX	The Three of Hearts
XX	The Ten of Spades
XXI	The Jack of Clubs
XXII	The Ten of Hearts
XXIII	The Six of Diamonds
XXIV	The Queen of Spades
XXV	The Four of Hearts
XXVI	The Ace of Clubs
XXVII	The King of Diamonds
XXVIII	The Five of Spades
XXIX	The Three of Diamonds
XXX	The Jack of Hearts
XXXI	The Queen of Hearts
XXXII	The Four of Clubs

XXXIII	The Ace of Spades
XXXIV	The Nine of Clubs
XXXV	The Five of Hearts
XXXVI	The Eight of Clubs
XXXVII	The Ten of Diamonds
XXXVIII	The Two of Hearts
XXXIX	The Six of Spades
XL	The Seven of Clubs
XLI	The Jack of Diamonds
XLII	The Four of Spades
XLIII	The Six of Hearts
XLIV	The Queen of Clubs
XLV	The Two of Diamonds
XLVI	The Nine of Spades
XLVII	The Ace of Diamonds
XLVIII	The Seven of Spades
XLIX	The Five of Diamonds
L	The Three of Clubs
LI	The King of Spades
LII	The Eight of Hearts

Note that the Nine of Hearts should come as near as possible to St Valentine's Day (14 February) and that the Nine of Spades properly belongs to the dreary month of November.

Reading the Cards: Third Method

The subject should shuffle the thirty-two cards, leaving out the Sixes, Fives, Fours, Threes, and Twoss, and cut them into three groups. Let the seer take up the first pack and ask the subject to pick out three cards. These are to stand for *the past*. The second group is then to be taken up and the subject will pick out five cards, to represent *the present*. From the third group seven cards are to be picked to represent *the future*. These are to be read in the light of the meanings given.

Further light may be thrown on the cards selected if each of the three, five, and seven cards respectively, are covered by one of the cards of smaller value. However, it is to be remembered that the 'fortune' proper is read in the cards selected, which include only those from the Sevens to the Aces.

To Wish (By Cards)

Define the wish in your own mind; shuffle the cards, keeping the Wish clearly before you.

Cut once, and note the card you cut.

Deal the whole pack into three lots or heaps.

Now take up each group and look for the card you cut. If it comes in the same lot as 'yourself', the answer is 'yes'.

If it comes with 'yourself' *and* if the Wish Card, the Nine of Hearts, is in the same lot, then it is 'yes', with great success or joy. If the Wish Card comes between 'yourself' and the card you cut, you will get your wish with Love.

If the Wish Card appears in the lot with 'yourself', but the card you cut is not in that group, this means you will not obtain what you actually wished for, but probably something that is better for you.

If the Nine of Spades comes in the same group with the card you cut, *and* 'yourself' also, a great disappointment is in store for you, although you *do* obtain this wish.

If the Nine of Spades comes with the card you cut,

and 'you' do not come in that group, you will not obtain what you want, but rather will feel bitter disappointment.

You do *not* get your wish unless 'you' and the card you cut while wishing are in the same group; and if there are many cards between these two cards, so much time will elapse before the wish comes true.

The nearer these two cards are to each other, when they are in the one lot, the sooner will the wish come true.

Note that something good involving a surprise is promised if the card you cut in order to know if you will get your wish by this method, happens to be the 'Card of the Week'.

Involved Meanings

Now learn the more involved meanings of each card. Note that, while some of these differ from the simple meanings you have learned already, they do not contradict them. When you can link both of them, you will be a really proficient card-reader.

Two of Spades

This card signifies a removal. If 'you' do not appear in the same 'set-out', you will hear of a friend whose removal will bring him or her nearer to you. It does not stand for a rich or very powerful friend. If reversed, it means that one you now call a friend will, before long, become your enemy.

But this meaning of an enemy in the guise of a friend more properly belongs to the meanings of small cards – those below the Sevens – when used to confirm or modify the meanings of the weightier cards – Sevens and upwards – around them. Thus, this Two of Spades coming up against the King of Hearts, a fairish or light-brown-haired-man – whom you can identify – shows he *is* your friend, though you may have been doubting him lately. The Two, if reversed, indicates that this particular friend is failing you in some way.

To hold two Twos gives you a small wish. Take advantage of it at once, noting whether the next card you turn up is black or red. If red, the answer is 'yes'. But if the black card is a Club it is not an unfavourable answer, though it stands for 'no'.

Note that cards of small value must always be interpretation in relation to the meanings of the weightier cards near them, and that if cut they stand for comparatively insignificant happenings.

Three of Spades

This card tells of a quarrel; but if 'you' are out with it, it is a quarrel in which you have the advantage. You are going to turn what looks like failure into success at the last minute. People who do this are never 'down' for long, especially if they *resolve to hold* all they gain.

This Three of Spades near the Ace of Hearts speaks of quarrels at home; if near the Ace of Spades it tells of business disputes. Near a Picture Card, it signifies anger with someone of that significance. But these are not important or angry quarrels, just disputes, contradictions, and foolish wrangling – irritation rather than passionate anger.

If reversed, this card tells of confusion, doubt, and apprehension. Delay any important enterprise if this card is in your hand, for the affair will be hindered by distrust and insecurity.

Four of Spades

If you cut this card, be prepared for sickness or for trouble in some form. This is not a good card. Even with good cards on both sides of it when it comes out in the 'set-out', it foretells loneliness and sadness of the heart. (An infallible cure for this evil is to go out and do someone a good turn!)

If reversed, This Four of Spades speaks definitely of a sick-bed. But if next to a Court Card of some other signification than 'yourself', the sickness will be for a person of that sex and colouring – yet it may be disastrous for you, in some way, that this person should be ill at this particular time.

Five of Spades

If you cut this Five of Spades, you are thereby warned to correct your bad temper! This is emphasised still more if it comes out in your 'fortune'.

You are jeopardising your own interest by indulging either your anger, jealousy or spite, or even hatred, unjustifiably.

Heed the warning and question yourself honestly: you may find that your anger is undeserved or your jealousy unwarranted.

If this Five of Spades comes out reversed, you will certainly be surprised, and not pleasantly so. This surprise also refers to the matter in which your anger has been misleading you.

It may be that this ugly little card promises you *mourning*. This is one of the least happy of its meanings. Be warned in time, or you will mourn indeed.

Six of Spades

This card says you will take a voyage or a journey towards water sooner than you expect. It will not be a prosperous journey nor one which you can make profitable. For Spades, even when they are not bad, stand for fatalistic things.

When it comes out near to Picture Cards, the Six of Spades tells of a voyage or of travelling towards the sea relating to some person or persons of the colour and sex indicated by the Court Card.

If reversed, this card warns you of a surprise in connection with a voyage or a place near water. It will not be a very unpleasant surprise, unless other Spades are on either side of this Six.

Seven of Spades

This card tells of a removal or change or upset, which you should avoid if possible. Spades are not a good suit, and Sevens stand for displacement or some kind of change.

If you cut this Seven reversed, be very watchful over your tongue and your temper, and look closely into the actions of all third parties concerning themselves with you and with one you love. For this card threatens the loss of one dear to you, with much trouble, if reversed – not a loss through death, but by estrangement or interference or because of the hate, malice, or jealousy of others.

This is never of good omen. If near to the Nine of Diamonds, you will hear of an accident; with the Nine of Spades also near, the person who has been injured may die.

Eight of Spades

This card stands for the night and illness, but if it comes out with good cards around it, some extraordinary things may happen in the night; yet your safety will not be seriously threatened. Between a King and Queen, this card foretells of a matrimonial separation; near but not separating them, a danger of trouble of this kind. Between two Kings, this Eight warns of the alienation of business friends. With the Nine of Diamonds, business trouble is still more clearly indicated.

If you have two Eights in your fortune, or if you cut two Eights in succession, you are advised to drop all idea of an illusion, or dream, or project, or ambition which attracts you at the present time. If you do not drop it, it will drop you, or fail you painfully. This warning applies especially to a 'Love Dream' – that is, the hope of attracting to yourself the love of a certain person who has no thought of you in connection with love. Women, in particular, should accept this warning of the two Eights if they wish to avoid rebuffs or slights which would hurt their feelings. However, a man should also heed the warning. If he is indulging in hopes which will not come to fruition, this warning may be valuable to him. The appearance of two Eights between Diamonds signify a false dream of money gains.

Spades, generally, have a sad significance, although with good cards near, they may speak only of delays to the happy events promised by the other cards.

Nine of Spades

If you cut this card at any time, your Luck is out. Do not try any new venture or tread any new ground until a week has passed. If you do, failure and disappointment will dog your footsteps.

If it lies between Heart cards, this ill-omened Nine of Spades tells of failure sweetened by Love. But if other Spades flank the Heart cards, it is illicit love and the end is evil! Between Diamonds, this Nine tells of poverty to be followed by riches. Between Clubs, of disappointment to be followed by success.

Next to, or near to, the Nine of Diamonds you will hear bad news of a death; next or near to the Seven of Diamonds then an accident, which may result in the death of the injured person.

Ten of Spades

This warns you of imminent unhappiness, grief, or sickness – perhaps of a mixture of all three evils!

If it comes in a 'set-out' with the Five of Spades before or after it, you are about to suffer a bereavement. With the Jack of Spades next to or near it when you have set out your cards, trouble or unrest is indicated. However, if it is held side by side with the other black Ten, a voyage – not necessarily an unhappy voyage – is surely going to be taken. Note that the two black Tens betoken a really long journey overseas, and not a mere cruise.

With the Nine of Diamonds, illness, probably accompanied by an operation is indicated. With the Nine of Spades flanking these, the sick person may be in considerable danger.

Jack of Spades

This is not a good card to cut, unless you are a very dark

unmarried man, when, it stands for 'yourself', and tells you to press forward with your plans – you are sure to win.

With another Knave he tells of deceit. Even if they are the two red Knaves, two Knaves represent deceit. Three Knaves together forecast dishonesty, swindling, often 'Big Business' frauds. Be warned – if you are connected with people whom you suspect of being far 'too clever' in business, cut your ties with them before they tarnish your good name or your credit. If your own affairs are safe, you will hear of unscrupulous dealings in financial circles when these three Knaves turn up together.

The Jack of Spades with the Queen of Spades, when both reversed, speaks of scandal. You will hear tell of domestic trouble among your married friends if you deal such a combination in your fortune.

If you cannot place a personal explanation on the Knave of Spades, he may stand for 'the night'. Thus, the King of Hearts and the Ten of Spades (sickness) warn you of a dear friend taken ill during the night, when this Knave is near them.

Queen of Spades

This card is generally taken to mean a very dark woman. However, if you the card reversed, it is taken to represent a malicious woman, one whom it is certainly not safe to trust. Alternatively it can signify a melancholy or bad-tempered person, either dark or fair. Be warned against such a woman, whatever her complexion, and say as little as possible when you are next in her company.

With her Jack, this Queen of Spades promises scandal as well as plots. Either a married woman of your acquaintance is playing with fire, or a married man is pursuing some woman other than his wife. In either case this combination indicates that the parties are running a considerable risk of being discovered.

There is a significant danger of scandal to 'you' if these two cards of evil omen – the Queen and Jack of Spades – are next or near to the Picture Card which signifies 'yourself'.

King of Spades

This card says you will hear of, or from, a public or 'Government man'; a man of affairs such as a banker, lawyer, stockbroker, head of a public department, or of a big firm; or perhaps he is a Member of Parliament?

If reversed, he is either troubled, worried, angry, or not so friendly to you as he was or as you believe him to be. Look to the cards next or near to him, in order to know more about this important man and his connection with your affairs. If reversed, and between Diamonds, he is bothered about money; between Hearts, about his domestic affairs – or yours, if the card signifying 'you' intervenes. The conjunction of Hearts with Spades stands for sensual pleasures. With Clubs, this card reversed, says that his ambition is slow in being rewarded; with other Spades disappointment or failure, or it may even be that death threatens him. This is certainly the case if the Nine of Spades touches him.

Ace of Spades

This card promises big business, especially if it subsequently appears with Diamonds near. If reversed, the

Ace of Spades warns you that news of a death is coming to you. If it is next to the Nine of Diamonds, it tells of a death caused by an accident.

The Ace of Spades with Hearts near implies sensual pleasures.

If this Ace comes between Hearts, you will be involved in a violent love affair. Next or near to the Nine of Clubs, you will go to a theatre. This Ace of Spades between a King and Queen signifies an illicit union or unlawful connection.

The Ace of Spades means a high building, probably an office block, when you are reading a fortune that is mainly concerned with business matters. This is especially so when the Ace of Hearts is out also. The two Aces will give you 'The Home' and 'The Office', but remember that two Aces always mean new plans of any description.

Two of Diamonds

This is one of the small cards which means a big thing. If you cut it, you will receive a considerable sum of money, and if it comes in your 'set-out', the money is as good as in your hands.

However, if reversed, with a Court Card near, its significance is: 'Do not keep your present engagement, whether it concerns money or love' – that is, the last engagement you made or the one you should otherwise keep within 24 hours of cutting this card. You will certainly be surprised or startled in the matter of this particular engagement, whether you keep it or not!

Three of Diamonds

This card says: 'Watch your domestic affairs'. If it comes out next to 'yourself', act with caution and prudence, for scandal is buzzing about you. This card says 'be discreet', or else it suggests that you should warn your partner to be more guarded as to his or her conduct.

If the unmarried cut this Three of Diamonds, it denotes that they will shortly be speaking with a friend, and quarrels concerning business or money or legal matters are likely to follow.

Four of Diamonds

This card indicates some kind of trouble through friends. The Four of Diamonds always stands for company, mixing with more people than usual, making new acquaintances. But this company is, as a rule, business or 'duty' company; it does not include socialising or celebration, though many Hearts around this card would modify this last meaning. In this case, business gathering *with* celebration is indicated. This does happen occasionally.

This Four of Diamonds has some kind of a warning of a secret betrayed. Hear everything and say nothing when you are in company after having cut this card.

Next to a Club, this card stands for a car – still with a warning!

Two Fours together convey a hint that you should check extravagance. When reversed they point to speculation. They do not say 'Cease to speculate', but only 'Be careful'.

Three Fours together are not a good omen. It indicates catastrophe of some sort. If you draw them, remember catastrophic events may still turn out well, in the long run.

Diamonds stand for things you cannot alter or help. Sit tight, keep your head cool, and cultivate the long view, if your fortune shows three Fours or even if you should cut them one after the other. In this latter case, only a warning as to probable catastrophe is the meaning.

Five of Diamonds

This card tells of a settlement with regard to some money matter with which you are concerned – not necessarily a large sum of money unless with other and larger Diamond cards, or with that important little money card, the Two of Diamonds, around. The settlement will be unexpected or you will have a surprise in connection with it.

In a set-out in which 'you' do not appear, the meaning is the same; but the settlement is not so directly for 'you', unless the card signifying yourself has been first cut. If reversed, this card signifies the law or legal proceedings and the successful ending is delayed.

Six of Diamonds

This card, when cut, speaks of hope and promises pleasure. But if it should be reversed, it threatens trouble from people beneath you, if you are in business.

If it comes up reversed in your 'fortune' and next to a King or a Queen, it says that the person denoted by the Picture Card will be widowed early in life.

The single man or woman who cuts it reversed, and finds it next or near to a Picture Card, will surely hear of the death of a dear friend's wife or husband; this will be an untimely death.

Seven of Diamonds

If you cut this card, you are thereby warned that friends – or some of those whom you look upon as friends – are speaking evil of you.

If the Jack of Hearts comes next or near to this card, you are going to hear of a birth. If the Jack and the Queen of Spades are in the same fortune by cards as this Seven, grave scandal is threatened.

The seven of Diamonds is not a good card.

Eight of Diamonds

The Eight of Diamonds stands for remarriage. If you cut it, you are either going to receive attentions from a widower, or to propose to a widow; or you are certain to hear of somebody making a second venture into matrimony.

Diamonds signify money. They also represent casual, haphazard, 'chancy' things. If you have made a deal involving money, this card promises success – but it is not a success 'you' can engineer or influence by any effort on your behalf. It speaks of hope but of *blind hope*. It gives no place to will or work.

If a Spade is next to this card, beware of danger or accident. However, if it is a Club, money and business are better. If it is a Heart, friendship helps greatly, especially if it is a Heart card of high significance.

Nine of Diamonds

This card foretells of unexpectedly good business, though it is business your skill cannot influence.

Yet the actual meaning of the Nine of Diamonds is anger, wounds, weapons; you must always read it in this connection if it appears in your fortune by cards. If next to, or near the Nine of Spades, you will hear of the death of a friend who has undergone an operation recently, or who has sustained an injury an accident.

Next to a Queen, this card tells of a woman who will undergo an operation; with Hearts near, it indicates that this will be successful. If near the Ten of Hearts, it tells of the safe birth of a child to a woman of the colouring of the Queen, who has, nevertheless, been in some danger. If the Nine of Diamonds is cut near two black Tens, the card tells of news of an operation on someone a great distance away. When the King of Diamonds comes up with it, he always represents a doctor; similarly, the King of Spades is a lawyer or banker, in this connection.

With Clubs near it, this Nine tells of anger over business matters, but they are not, otherwise, unfortunate business matters. With the Ace of Spades, a serious quarrel over business.

Ten of Diamonds

It is a very auspicious sign to cut this card. The Ten of Diamonds stands for money; a good round sum of money, although not the largest sum you can receive, in connection with any deal or business venture in which you are interested. The little Two of Diamonds means a larger sum still.

Two Red Tens together signify a lucky surprise in connection with money. But if both are reversed, you will be in touch with prosperous and charming people who are over-inclined to look on the wine when it is red.

Resolve not to share in their excesses.

Jack of Diamonds

This card says you may look for important written communications.

For a very fair or red-headed bachelor to cut it, his luck is in – he may do big things, and these will undoubtedly turn out well, for this Knave stands for 'himself'.

If next to another Picture Card, the sex and colouring of the sender of the weighty messages may be deduced.

The matter of the letter or communication may be read from adjacent cards. Hearts signify things social and of romantic attachment; Spades, sickness or anxiety; Diamonds, money; Clubs, stand for things that have been long desired and fought for.

Queen of Diamonds

This card signifies either a very fair or a red- or white-haired woman. If you are a fair girl, it is 'you', and it is always exceptionally lucky either to cut 'yourself' or to have the card of your own signification come out. It means that you can control any matter in which you are interested; that you may *act* this week, without fear. If you are married, the King of Diamonds is your husband, whatever colour your husband may actually be. If you are *not* a fair woman, this represents a good woman of that complexion unless she comes up with Spades. If she is reversed, she is a flirt and is unreliable.

With the King of Diamonds, this tells of a married couple; but if the Nine of Hearts is with them, you will hear of the engagement of this fair woman very shortly. Any Diamond Court Card with the Nine of Clubs, says you have a rival in love.

King of Diamonds

If you cut this card, you will certainly have reason to see a doctor or you will have some business with a medical man. The business does not necessarily signify anxiety – to cut a Picture Card always indicates friends; Kings are generally powerful friends.

This King of Diamonds stands for a very fair man, a red-haired man or a grey-headed one.

If reversed, he may be an enemy or a treacherous person. More frequently, an enemy in business. You see how true it is that Diamonds are 'chancy' things. When they mean good fortunes, there is an element of uncertainty about it. Yet Diamonds stand for the morning and for youth and hope too. But these are uncertain and impermanent.

Ace of Diamonds

When this card is cut, it indicates that you can expect to receive money through the post; cheques, notes, etc. When reversed, it tells that a letter about money, perhaps containing news of money, is being delayed although it *is* coming to you. Next to a Court Card, the money comes from a person of the sex and colouring of the Court Card's meaning.

If the Ace of Diamonds is with the King and the Nine of Hearts, it promises you the offer of a ring and says that you will make a prosperous marriage; of course that is if 'you' are also held in the hand. If 'you' are absent, the monied marriage is for the person indicated by the surrounding cards. Or it will be within your reach but you look on the opportunity with indifference.

Two of Hearts

A visit from a lover. If reversed, the opposition to a love affair; or, if with Clubs, the opposition of those who love you to some project with which you want to push on.

A man or woman in business may expect someone who loves him or her to come to the home, office or place of work.

Three of Hearts

This card promises success, but if reversed you may be careful that your own imprudence in the past, in connection with seeking this change, does not cause you sorrow.

With another Heart near it in your 'set-out' of cards, the Three of Hearts tells of achievement. Next to a Picture Card, of a kiss from a person of the sex and complexion shown by the Court Card.

Two Threes side by side tell of victory in connection with some comparatively small matter about which you have been anxious. Two Red Threes, of joy with the victory. But if one of the two Threes is a black Spade, there will be jealousy, which will take some of the pleasure from your triumph.

Four of Hearts

Although this card means a messenger, it stands for stubbornness in connection with a matter on which you will receive a message.

If next or near to 'yourself' (the Picture Card signifying 'you') you are being stubborn about some matter on which you are pushing to get your own way because it *is* your own way and not because it is the right way. Ask yourself if it would not be better to put your obstinacy aside and begin again?

If next or near to the card which signifies the person on whom you have fixed your affection, this person will be hard to win indeed! But Hearts cannot carry a really bad meaning. This comparatively insignificant Four of Hearts may serve to convey a message, having some reference to stubbornness – a stubborn aim or a stubborn person rather than a really persevering one.

Five of Hearts

This card has to do with married love, but it promises that the subject will suffer through jealousy. If cut in the week to which it belongs, this Five of Hearts tells you that you are sure to receive a present before long. But if it comes out next to a Ten of any suit, an invitation is promised.

Near a King and Queen, you are going to be surprised by news of a marriage. If near Diamonds, a good change in money matters is promised. If the Five of Hearts is near any Clubs, you will reap the result of your efforts and of your perseverance in the past – the amount will be according to the number or dignity of the cards. As a general rule, though, cards of small value rarely promise big events or successes.

Six of Hearts

Speaks of the reappearance in your life of an old lover or of someone who, long ago, paid you attention – this person will proceed to court you in earnest now. When reversed, this Six of Hearts tells of some attempt to trick you. It is not a villain who will try to do this, but a rather good-hearted though distinctly 'tricky' person. We all know this type – people who would rather run crook-edly than straight, even when to go straight would be less trouble! Look out for such a person and ignore any attempt they might make to rush you into a particular line of action.

Let 'masterly inactivity' be your motto. If properly carried out, you cannot be beaten while you practise this policy.

Seven of Hearts

This card tells us of something that is not lasting – a gain in money matters which will be fairly short-lived, or an increase in one's income which will not be as good as it first sounds. It may be a small success in con-nection with social affairs – something temporary. Look at the cards on each side to find out more about the matter.

If reversed, the Seven of Hearts tells of the jealousy of women. Again, the matter on which this jealousy turns must be interpreted from the cards that surround it. However, although they *may* refer to passion, Hearts are never entirely bad.

Eight of Hearts

This card, which belongs to the last week in the dying year, tells of a mind at ease and of a good, friendly feel-ing surrounding you. The key-significance of this Eight of Hearts is *thoughts* – happy thinking, generous think-ing; and this is indeed a good sign to close the passing year and with which to open the unknown days of the New Year.

This Eight has a further message of happy spending, perhaps of buying new clothes which will please you. Next or near to the Ace of Diamonds, the meaning is an engagement ring in the coming year, with happy spending of money in furniture, dress, etc., in the immediate time following on the engagement. Further, it implies company, feasting, and so on.

Note that, while Eight is the number of movement and change, the good omen of the Hearts is stronger that the uncertainty indicated by the number. Happy changes, due to love, are promised by this Eight of Hearts, whatever week in the year it is cut or dealt out in the 'set-out'.

Nine of Hearts

This is the best card in the pack. It stands, first and foremost, for love; happy love, success in love or triumphant love. Therefore, it is fittingly associated with the Feast of St Valentine, the patron of true lovers. This fateful date is was celebrated long before it became the name-day of the gentle Christian saint. St Valentine's Day is actually the old Roman feast of the *Lupercalia*, of the goddess of fertility, of the blooming of life.

This Nine of Hearts also stands for success. If you cut it in the first half of February, or if it is dealt to you, be sure to 'wish on it' as you touch it. You will succeed in love, if love is what you are keen on at the moment. Success with money is indicated if Diamonds are on either side, when you tell your fortune. Success in your ambitions is indicated if Clubs are near this lucky card. With the Knave of Hearts it denotes an engagement. With a King and Queen of the same suit, a wedding. These combinations with the Ace of Hearts tell of an engagement or a wedding at your home. With the card that signifies 'you', the engagement or the wedding is for you. This card near the Ace of Hearts promises a celebration at your house.

Ten of Hearts

The Ten of Hearts promises domestic and family happiness – a good change if there has been recent anxiety in connection with social or financial matters. The Ten of Hearts neutralises the effects of evil cards near it, and it strengthens and confirms good omens. This is its *general* meaning.

The Ten of Hearts has a more particular significance associated with pleasure, a place of amusement or a party. If a Ten of Hearts comes next to the Ace of Spades, you are going to a theatre; next to a King, to a dinner party; next to a Queen, a formal evening function, if you are a man. The Ten of Hearts next to a Queen, in a fortune by cards told for a woman, tells her that she can expect to receive something very pleasant through the post. Between a Queen and a King, the card signifies a happy event, an addition to the family, is foretold. Next to a Queen, a very ardent lover; for a single man, a sweetheart who is *young*.

The Ten of Hearts promises *change*, but it is invariably a very good change which is indicated.

Jack of Hearts

This card speaks of love and the thoughts of the loved one which are active about you.

The Knave of Hearts stands for one who is beloved,

of either sex. It promises a young man or woman a speedy and happy engagement. If it is next or near to the Nine of Diamonds, it tells of a quarrel with the beloved; if next or near to the Nine of Spades, it speaks of misfortune to the loved one.

If those who are not concerned with love and love-making cut this card, or it comes out in their 'fortune', it promises them much joy through the natural affections of the heart, which belong to every age and time of life.

Queen of Hearts

It is very lucky indeed for a woman with warm golden or chestnut hair to cut this card, for it stands for 'herself' and promises her that she may safely embark on any enterprise with sure hopes of success. She may also accept any opportunity that presents itself.

When this card comes out as part of the fortune, it means that the subject will hear news of a woman of the colouring represented. If it appears next to the Jack of Hearts, there will be news of an engagement; on one side of the Nine of Hearts, with the King on the other side, a happy marriage. The King and Queen of any suit mean, for a business man, a partnership or agreement. The Queen of Hearts next to the Ace of Spades stands for an actress. If it is reversed, there will be news of a handsome but changeable woman, rather than an affectionate woman, which the card represents when it comes out the right way up.

King of Hearts

This is an extraordinarily good card for anyone. If it should be cut for a married man of this colouring – fairish or light brown – there is scarcely anything he may not dare to do.

The King of Hearts with the Nine of Hearts tells of an engagement; with the Ten of Hearts, indicating a happy marriage.

Two Kings together in your fortune by cards signify an important business meeting which is being held about this time and which will ultimately increase your financial prosperity. Two Kings reversed say that new business ventures must be closely watched if they are to prove successful. (Remember, you can only read King as 'reversed' if you have put 'R' for reversed in the top, left-hand corner.) If you do not specifically identify the King of Hearts as a relative, friend or lover, its general meaning is of a good, loving man, with a rather hasty temper. If reversed, this indicates that he is inclined to be fickle.

Note that the King of Hearts must always stand for the husband of a married woman who is 'between colours', when her cards are being read, whatever colour her husband may be.

Ace of Hearts

This card stands for the house. If reversed, it stands for a change of residence, a holiday or merely 'a strange bed' for a night or two for the person whose cards are being read.

A keen businessman or woman may take the Ace of Hearts to mean the office.

A Picture Card near and facing towards the Ace, means that a person of the sex and colouring indicated by the picture is coming to your house; facing away from the Ace, such a person is going away from the place. With the Ace of Spades near, the visit concerns business. The Ten of Hearts near this Ace indicates a party or a celebration in your home. When the Knave and Nine of Hearts are near, this indicates an engagement for someone in the home; the King with the Ten promises a wedding. A red King with his Queen also indicates a wedding; a black King and Queen show a partnership. If these are Spades, the business of the partnership will involve some anxiety.

The Queen and Knave of Spades near the Ace of Hearts tell of scandalous conduct. Two Kings in the same fortune as this card show an important business conference. Depending on how near they are near to the Ace, this will mean more success for the subjects domestic or professional interests.

Two of Clubs

This card stands for letters. The cards of small value – Sixes and under – are not important, but the smallest cards have their meanings, and these should be read in conjunction with the cards that lie alongside of them. This card says you are going to handle important letters. With two Kings the letters will be about a business meeting; with two Queens, about committee meetings or other mundane gatherings. With the Ace of Spades and the Nine of Clubs, letters about a theatre or a theatrical venture. But the letters decide nothing. This small card promises nothing definite.

Two Twos together in a hand of cards warn you to exercise self-control in a matter that will soon be in progress. Three Twos convey a hint of treachery; while four Twos tell you to expect very striking developments concerning a matter, though small and unimportant enough in itself.

Three of Clubs

If you cut this card, your position, with regard to some matter which had threatened it, has been stabilised. But you will do well to practise economy, for you are not yet out of the woods nor quite secure in your holding or position or job. If this card comes out in a 'set-out' among pictures, you will hear of one of your friends making a second marriage late in life; a very prudent, worldly-wise 'look-to-the-future' sort of arrangement it will be. To identify the blushing elderly bride or bridegroom, look to the Picture Card next or near to this Three.

Among reversed cards, this Three of Clubs stands for quarrelling about a post or worldly affairs – small and rather insignificant affairs, for the Three is a small number. But Clubs always stand for effort, success, 'getting there', and when they are reversed only delay is indicated.

Four of Clubs

This card promises pleasures, but only on a small or insignificant scale, and with some relation to business. If reversed, the Four of Clubs speaks of delays to a pleasure already arranged, or perhaps of some little hitch in the arrangements. Next to a Picture Card in a 'set-out', this card promises a journey or a business deal, involving a car or cars, with a person of the sex and colouring indicated by the Picture Card.

To anyone involved in important business, this card

says: 'Be prudent and you will succeed; but the success you gain will bring you satisfaction rather than a real increase in money.'

Five of Clubs

This card suggests a new lover. If the cards around it are of small value, an engagement or marriage with the stranger is not promised. If Spades are near, guard yourself against treachery or deception from someone professing a regard for you.

A girl cutting it reversed may indeed walk warily. A man who cuts this card will find that a lady whom he looks upon as a friend has a wish to be something more – she wants to tempt him from his present commitment.

If reversed and set between a King and Queen of the same suit, this card tells you of matrimonial reactions disturbing married friends. But with good cards around, the rift will not widen; they will 'kiss again with tears'.

Six of Clubs

This card promises gifts. It bodes well for your ambition, too, but with bad cards near, it warns you *against* someone who is soon to give you a valuable present.

If near the Ace of Diamonds in a young person's hand, it tells of the gift of a ring; for older people a valuable present of something *round* – a bracelet, a belt, or an oval cigarette-case or tie-band. Yet one should always read of this present in connection with ambition or business.

Two Sixes tell of gain, and even though they might be reversed, they promise a joy of some kind.

Three Sixes promise that you will soon be in touch with

a very generous person. If they come up with the card representing 'yourself', you are being very generous.

Seven of Clubs

This card is one of the best in the pack. It stands for *victory*.

If you are concerned as to the result of any business, or affair, or contest, you may confidently expect the very best.

If reversed, its meaning is not quite so good, the significance, then being *financial worry*; but note that this is not loss or even disappointment, only worry; at worst, it is *delay* which causes the worry.

Clubs are always good in relation to business inquiries, though they do not mean things are easy to come by. This card promises no mere good luck, but victory by your own efforts.

Eight of Clubs

This card promises you the help of a good friend or ally, of the opposite sex to your own.

In the 'fortune' of a business man, this Eight of Clubs, if there is a King or Kings near it, may mean a new partner in business. However, when reversed it tells of a warning against speculation, a warning which a *real* friend has already given you.

If it comes near black cards or Hearts, your new friend is a person either of dark or of light-brown complexion; with Diamonds near, he or she will be fair or grey.

This Eight of Clubs is a happy sign for lovers in distress. It tells of the goodwill of a friend able and willing to help. Reversed, it shows one not so powerful, though very willing to make the course of true love run more smoothly.

Nine of Clubs

This card tells you that you are going to hear of a legacy or of some business following the validation of a will. If it is cut reversed, it speaks of delayed and troubled journeys, generally after or connected with a death or a funeral.

With the Jack of Spades, business with a lawyer is promised. With either the King, Queen, or Jack of Diamonds, rivalry in love is sure to crop up.

To an unmarried man or woman, this card, if cut, says: 'Do not act against the wishes of your friends.' However, to the married and to all those who are concerned with business or with secret affairs, the contrary advice is indicated: 'Take no advice but your own and you will do well.'

Ten of Clubs

This is a very good card to cut if business affairs are engrossing you. It says: 'Cease to worry.' Things are going better than you fear. It does not promise a dramatically good change, but a sure and certain improvement. 'The slow success is the sure success' – especially in business.

This card often foretells of a journey, concerned with good business rather than pleasure. With the other black Ten, a voyage is certain, and successful if red cards are around these two black ones.

All Clubs signify ambition, success which has been slow and difficult to come by, manhood, decisiveness, and the more masculine qualities of the mind.

Two Tens indicate a change of trade. Two red Tens say a lucky and surprising change concerning your business. Three Tens stand for prosperity and the promise of a happy future.

Jack of Clubs

It is very lucky indeed to cut this card at any time. To a dark young girl, it promises a faithful lover and a marriage founded on true friendship and mutual esteem. To a dark young bachelor, it says: 'Go on as you are now doing. You are surely working towards success.' If an older, dark man cuts it, or if it comes in a fortune told him, this Jack of Clubs bids him follow out the thought which at present grips him; in short, to act on his own initiative. An older, married woman who cuts the Jack of Clubs will hear gratifying news of her son's success.

For those who are not of the dark-brown complexion of which Clubs are the signification, this Jack of Clubs says that a friend is thinking about them and they will certainly hear of him – a hasty, big-hearted friend; not necessarily a man friend, but a very true one of either sex.

If a brown-eyed person's fortune is being read, the seer may make the card that particular person's 'thoughts', and if carefully noting the cards around this one, will be able to tell much of the hopes, aspirations and ambitions, as distinct from the actual events in the subject's life, at the time.

Queen of Clubs

If you are a dark-eyed, brown-haired girl or woman, it is very lucky to cut this card, for it signifies 'yourself'. It says: 'Go in and win! Be bold, be bold, and evermore be bold!' You will surely come out on top, whatever tight corner you are in.

If you are a man of this colouring, the omen is lucky in regard to love. For whatever the colouring of the woman you love might be, this card stands for her; she is *your* Queen and she is thinking sweet thoughts of you. However, if reversed, you have offended her or she is unhappy; ensure that you rectify this situation as soon as possible.

King of Clubs

It is always lucky to cut this card because the Clubs stand for successful efforts and Kings are powerful helpers.

The Club Picture Cards signify good friends rather than lovers, unless you are a dark woman (Queen of Clubs). This card reversed means that your powerful friend is worried or hindered – not *quite* so powerful on your behalf. With Spades near there is trouble between you. If a man holds it with the Queen near, a powerful partnership is suggested; with the wish card (Nine of Hearts) near, great success throughout the year. If cut with the Ten of Hearts, then marriage with someone you now regard as a friend is indicated. This last applies to either a man or a woman.

Ace of Clubs

This card signifies important papers, written plans, shares, contracts, leases – lucky, successful papers, in fact, rather than mere letters. Good business letters *may* be indicated.

If reversed, this card means a delay to written prospects or a delay over signed papers, with perhaps some anxiety as to the outcome.

However, unless surrounded by Spades, even if the Ace is reversed, it does not necessarily mean unpleasant communications regarding business.

Clubs always refer to ability, merit, and things that have been earned or deserved.

Tea-leaf Fortunes

The secret of success in this art consists of concentration, which enables the seer, who has a mind empty of all outside matters, to seize at a glance the symbols thrown up in the teacups and to read them intelligently so that the subject, or person whose cup is being read, can understand.

The cup must be passed directly to the seer by the person who has drunk the tea. If the cup passes from hand to hand before it reaches the seer, the fortune will be confused and undefined, and most likely untrue.

It is also desirable that the subject should sit near the seer when the cup has been given up. But the cup ought to be turned over on to the saucer to allow for 'tears' to be drained off the leaves before it is handed to the seer. It is extraordinary how tears, or drops of tea, will stay in the cup, however long it has remained turned over on the saucer, if there is matter for grief in the fortune of the subject.

Some subjects turn the cup round three times and touch the edge of the saucer with the cup, 'wishing the wish of the heart' as they do so. But unless there is a clear or outstanding star near the top on the inner side of the teacup, no more is heard of this 'wish of the heart'. (Wishes properly belong to card-reading.)

The seer or reader picks up the turned-over cup from the saucer, which the subject hands over.

You (if 'you' are the seer) hold the cup in your right hand. Note that the handle of the teacup is the house or home of the subject or 'place'. For someone whose interest is entirely in business, the handle may stand for 'the office'; for an actress it may mean 'the theatre', for a doctor, 'the surgery'. But for the average man or woman you will do well to read it as 'the home'.

The near or inner side of the cup, as you hold it in your right hand, is 'the fortune', the things that are happening or are sure to happen.

On the outer or farther side we read thoughts, things that may come, that are likely or possible but that are now very much 'in the air', unfulfilled, uncertain. If you read the same person's cup tomorrow or in a week's time, there may be quite a different story to be read from the outer side of the cup.

Some seers read a month's time in the depths of the cup, dividing it into two and reading the immediate fortnight that is coming from the top half, and the third and fourth weeks from now in the lower half of the cup's side. Happenings of a month ahead are near the bottom of the side. The very top is today. The rim is now. Close to the rim is by first post tomorrow morning. A leaf or sprig sticking out on the rim, startling news, now. Any sign sticking out implies surprise, even shock.

Note that the leaves or sprigs of tea dust – any combination of symbols, in fact – that lie on the bottom of the cup stand for trouble, annoyance, anxiety, mishap, bad luck, misfortune. Even if it is a star, it is a wish or a 'glory' that will cause the subject more sorrow than joy. And drops, moisture, liquid, things that stand for 'tears' always cling to the bottom of the cup. Notice especially that whatever you read in the bottom of the cup is timed as *now*. This is all to the good. Your subject's cup may be quite clear at the bottom tomorrow!

Sometimes, especially if the seer is reading a person's cup for the first time, and more especially if they are meeting for the first time, the skilled reader will rule out all 'time' and will read from the cup a fortune that goes far ahead and may cover the whole life of the subject.

The most experienced reader of teacups cannot tell what it is that impels him or her to do this, but does know that he or she is actually and truly reading what is sure to come true, and feels, with the feeling that is stronger than all knowledge, that what is 'seen' must be said. This rare and inexplicable state of mind looks beyond all symbolism. Symbols are no longer there; for the seer is now really clairvoyant, seeing nothing, but 'telling' of what is surely in the veiled future.

The meaning of the symbols

All the signs explained here are to be read as important or negligible according to size and clearness. Signs that disappear almost as they are read are true things that are ceasing to matter.

animals horses and dogs are friends. A lion represents a powerful friend. A tiger is an unreliable rich man, not necessarily an enemy. Leopards and wolves are enemies. A cat or a cow is a deceitful woman. Monkeys are mischievous people, especially if they are grinning.

baby a sign that one may be expected. If a cradle is near it, all will be well.

birds if they are in flight, birds say that news is coming. A bird standing is not such a good sign. A bird standing on one leg indicates plans frustrated or things changed for the worse since news was received.

circles *see* RINGS.

crosses symbolise things earned. A large, well-made cross tells of painful ambition realised. A small or ill-made cross implies obstacles, with danger of losses. A cross beside a grave, a funeral. Near to a wreath of flowers, a death. Not 'near' if there are no tears in the bottom of the cup.

dots are news, but of things of the mind, scholarship, science. Dots set as a triangle denote a wish, a successful but not exactly a material one. Dots are 'fine' things, sometimes ideas. Dots set inside small circles are money through business or affairs.

faces these are described to the subject, saying whether they stand for men or women, old or young, sad or joyful people. The subject must identify them. Sometimes the subject's own face is formed clearly by dots. Notice its position and the signs near it. But the fact that it is there, means that the day or the time is important.

gardens represent flirtations.

hearts two hearts tell of an engagement. If there is a ring around them or near them, this denotes a happy marriage. A crown over the joined hearts is a very auspicious sign.

letters denote the arrival of something by post. A dot in the middle of a square or 'long square' letter, tells of money by post.

letters of the alphabet alphabet letters are often thrown up in the teacup with astonishing clarity. These do not always stand for the initials of a name; they may indicate a town. But two or three capital letters together are, as a rule, the initials of someone with whom the subject ought to get into communication. Figures must be read in conjunction with the symbols that are near to it.

lines lines stand for distance. Two lines are journeys by train or car. A ship is a voyage. Cars, engines and such things stand for themselves, but notice how they are placed and where.

masses or **heaps** masses or heaps of tea leaves are prosperity. The larger or higher they are, the more money or good luck is indicated. But masses in the bottom of the cup indicate that there is much anxiety even concerning what should be unmitigated good.

rings if they are small, rings mean business offers; if large, a proposal of marriage. Rings are always something that involves a question or an offer. A circle with a letter near it says the offer will be made in writing.

A ring formed of dots denotes an offer that is not so definite. A half or a part circle, not fully closed, is an indefinite offer or a half-question thrown out as a 'feeler' or with some hesitation. The same rule applying to smallness or largeness applies to the complete ring. It denotes business if small and marriage if large.

sprigs stand for people. Tightly curled sprigs are men, and more loosely furled ones are women. When upstanding, these are straightforward people, although if there is any kind of a weapon pointed at them, or from them, the message is 'Beware'. Sprigs set across are people who have been vexed. Look at the nearby symbols to find out why. Sprigs set sideways are people who are not quite trustworthy. People are also represented by faces, initials and signs, which the subject must identify.

squares tell of safety from a feared danger or deliverance.

With a half-moon, squares denote danger of drowning escaped. But squares say that the subject is, for the time being, 'taking one step forward and two steps backwards' and, at best, is merely 'marking time', even if the square is set in the clear of the cup's side.

stars indicate successes, desires fulfilled, 'glory' achieved and startling success. If they appear in the bottom, something in the nature of fatality accompanies the good happenings.

triangles symbolise prevention of ill or trouble avoided. Look at the symbols nearby to interpret these more fully.

Enough has been said to show how the teacups ought to be read. 'The way to do it, is to do it.' A last word to the would-be seer: Never hesitate to say what you see clearly in the cup you are reading.

If you are sincere (selfless) in the matter and the subject is intelligent and anxious to know things, what you say is sure to be true or to come true.

Dice and Good Luck

Dice have been used for many games of chance and fortune throughout history. From ancient Egypt and classical Greece to the Far East, numbered cubes made of wood, glass, ivory or metal with their sides inscribed from 1–6 were popular for games and as a means of consultation. It was found through their medium that future happenings and events could be predicted.

Test this ancient form of fortune-telling:

Draw a chalk ring on the table or tablecloth. Three new dice and a new cup or shaker box are needed. All three dice must be shaken in the box, with the box held in the left hand.

If you throw all the dice outside this ring, ask no more, and, above all, steer clear of quarrels! One or two of the dice falling outside the ring indicates the same warning in a milder form. But the thrower, in this case, may throw again.

The following are the common interpretations of the sum total of the numbers on the faces that fall uppermost:

one (that is one dice with one point and two with blanks) says 'Nothing doing!'

two slight trouble, and rather a lack of good news. Nothing to worry about.

three good. Seize the chance that comes *today*. Your wish will be fulfilled, or a pleasing or happy event will take place.

four a disappointment; but it will turn out to be for the best.

five news of a death, but no surprise about the news.

six a marriage, news of which will surprise if not distress the thrower. Also a sign of the loss of a portion of wealth.

seven an omen of good luck. All will go well in the matter about which you are now anxious.

eight disagreeable news through the post. 'Sit tight'. Better news will follow.

nine this is a good throw. It is a sign of good happenings but with some touch of scandal. Success in love or reconciliation of a quarrel or disagreement could also occur.

ten uncertainty, but nothing worse. 'Wait till the clouds roll by.'

eleven danger of loss of money through treachery. This also indicates the illness of someone close.

twelve someone seeks to involve you in an intrigue. Refuse to grant favours that are asked of you. There is danger of you being made a cat's paw. Do not act without seeking advice from a friend.

thirteen warns you that an enemy seeks your downfall. Throw again, and if the number is higher, he or she will not succeed.

fourteen long voyaging but not yet. Your travels will prove profitable but not easily. Always have hope. This is also an indication of a new friendship to come.

fifteen some domestic trouble. Examine whether there are people making mischief in your home. Sort it out!

sixteen you are going to be lucky in a matter of which you are not hopeful. Tell no one of your gains for a week after you know of them. Sixteen also warns you not to think too much about money. Other important things are being neglected by you. You will not want for money ever, but it will not supply the need of friendship.

seventeen indicates something very good indeed, unearned, unsought, even undeserved. You may well be thankful when this comes. Perhaps a suggestion or proposal from a stranger.

eighteen this is the very best throw of all. It tells of a high destiny, great luck and happiness. But beware of inconstancy when your luck is at its highest. 'The full cup needs a steady hand.'

Fortune Telling
by Numbers

Many of us think of ourselves as having 'lucky numbers'. We attach significance to some numbers for personal reasons, for example, those that are associated with
addresses, ages or dates of important events. Every time
we buy a lottery ticket we hope that these are the lucky
numbers that are going to change our lives. But, there is
also a fun way of divining the numbers that could play a
part in your fortune.

Numbers have a major part to play in our lives. They
are everywhere! There are quite simple ways of identifying the special number that brings you luck on a certain day.

That a certain amount of character and fortune may
be revealed by means of figures is a fact that can be tested
for itself. The results achieved by this method of divination are truly astonishing, and can be very rewarding to
the mathematician in the attempt to solve the riddle of
human nature.

Certain groups of figures stand for different qualities. Those given in the table following are only a small
portion of the whole, but they are sufficient for the
beginner. Each letter of the alphabet has its accompanying digit, and each digit has its abstract condition:–

A	1	Passion, ambition, design
B	2	Destruction, death
C	3	Religion, destiny, the soul
D	4	Solidity, sagacity, power
E	5	The stars, happiness, graces, marriage
F	6	Perfect labour
G	7	Course of life, repose, liberty, success
H	8	Justice, preservation
I	9	Imperfection, grief, pain, expectation
J	600	Perfection
K	10	Success, reason, future happiness
L	20	Austerity, sadness
M	30	Fame, a wedding
N	40	Fetes, a wedding
O	50	Pardon, liberty
P	60	Widowhood
Q	70	Science, the graces
R	80	A cure
S	90	Blindness, error, affliction
T	100	Divine favour
U	200	Irresolution
V	700	Strength
W	1400	Perfection of strength
X	300	Safety, belief, philosophy
Y	400	Long and wearisome journey
Z	500	Holiness
	800	Empire
	900	War, combats, struggles

The first thing to ask is the name of the subject. He writes it on a slip of paper, and next to each letter its accompanying figure. Here is the name, Dick James Smith:–

D	4	J	600	S	90
I	9	A	1	M	30
C	3	M	30	I	9
K	10	E	5	T	100
		S	90	H	8

Now they are added separately:–

Dick = 26 James = 726   Smith = 237

Add the three totals together:–

Dick	26
James	726
Smith	237
	989

The interpretation:–

900	War, combats, struggles
80	A cure
9	Imperfection, grief, pain, expectation.

The deduction being that Dick James Smith is endowed with a quarrelsome, headstrong nature, optimism, and inefficient willpower, which are destined to cause him trouble, loss, and misery.

Should the total of the names reach beyond 1390, the first digit must be subtracted, for example as in the name, Johannah Christine Whiting:–

J	600	C	3	W	1400
O	50	H	8	H	8
H	8	R	80	I	9
A	1	I	9	T	100
N	40	S	90	I	9
N	40	T	100	N	40
A	1	I	9	G	7
H	8	N	40		
		E	5		
	748		344		1573

Total = 2665, take away the first figure, leaves 665.

600   Perfection

60   Widowhood.

5   The stars, happiness, graces, marriage.

The analysis showing that Johannah Christine Whiting's life will be a mixture of joy and sorrow, the latter borne by a courageous and tranquil spirit. Her integrity and attractiveness of character will, no doubt, bring her much love and friends.

If the fortune-teller has a good memory, the table of qualities can be memorised, and a great aid to this is to practise with it perhaps analysing an author, statesman, or friend.

The fortune-teller's own name should reveal the fundamental truths of this method, and the analysis of people from history will show the distinguishing traits that have made them famous. For example, take Florence Nightingale:—

F	6	N	40
L	20	I	9
O	50	G	7
R	80	H	8
E	5	T	100
N	40	I	9
C	3	N	40
E	5	G	7
		A	1
		L	20
		E	5
	209		246

Total = 455

400   Long and wearisome voyage
50   Pardon and liberty
5   The stars, happiness, graces.

The numbers of the alphabet

1	2	3	4	5	6	7	8	9
A	B	C	D	E	F	G	H	I
J	K	L	M	N	O	P	Q	R
S	T	U	V	W	X	Y	Z	

Now suppose your name is Gladys Templeton, write it downwards, like this:

G	7	T	2
L	3	E	5
A	1	M	4
D	4	P	7
Y	7	L	3
S	1	E	5
		T	2
		O	6
		N	5

Total = 62

You have added to each letter the number that stands for it. Their total value added together is 62. These two numbers add up to 8. You may bank on the importance of this 8, though there are some numerologists who would add to it certain mystic numbers which represent the day on which you make the calculation. The above is simple and it works out, strange to say, with striking results!

Finding your lucky number

Suppose you were born on the 16th June 1971:
Take the date of the month = 16

Add the figures together $(1 + 6)$ = 7
June is the sixth month, so add   6
Add the year of your birth   1971
_____
                                1984
_____
Add these figures together:–
   $(1 + 9 + 8 + 4)$ =   22 and
   22 (*ie.* 2 and 2)   =   4

275

You will find that the figure 4 will turn out well for you; also any figures or any number in which it appears; or any of its multiples 8, 12, 16, as well as 49, 48, 94, 84; and especially 40, for the 0 intensifies any figure which it comes after.

Note that number 4 itself is not a very good number, although it will be favourable for you. People whose number is 4 suffer from 'temper' – their own, as well as that of other people! To live in a house that is Number 4, to get a bus or train or theatre ticket in which 4 appears, more especially if the whole adds up to 4 or to a multiple of 4 – this means happy travelling, auspicious enterprises. Wednesday being the fourth day of the week, will be lucky; April, the fourth month in the year also, especially if these be the day or the month of your birth.

But should you particularly dislike this number 4, it is up to you to change it. Some people add the day of the week's number to those given, Sunday being number 1, Monday number 2, and so on. This plan, if you adopt it, gives you a different number. You may work them both together, using one for business and the other for personal luck. But do not change entirely from 4, if this number is serving you well.

Fortune Telling by Dominoes

Each small oblong domino has a secret meaning. It is a simple matter to commit these to memory; and in this, as in other methods of divination, the fundamental principle is that of comparison and calculation.

The dominoes used range from double-six to double-blank, and these symbolise the various conditions of fate likely to befall mankind. The exponent places the dominoes on the table, and, having turned them face down proceeds to shuffle them. When this is done, the subject is requested to draw three pieces, one at a time. Between the choice of each, the dominoes should be shuffled.

The first supplies an impression; should it be drawn a second time, the impression becomes a conviction. The third, however, may lessen or wholly contradict its degree of importance, and this is where calculation and comparison in blending the signs are essential to a successful justification and interpretation of these symbols.

Do not draw more than three pieces at a single consultation or you may well find that interpretations are misleading.

Double-six is an emblem of matrimonial happiness and financial prosperity.

Six-five is almost equally fortunate. Perseverance and concentration are rewarded by ultimate success.

Six-four implies a comfortable income, and secures happiness in marriage.

Six-three demonstrates that fate smiles upon love and marriage of the subject.

Six-two shows prudence, hard work, and a certain amount of good luck, or exposure and shame for any wrong-doing.

Six-one promises two marriages to the young subject, the first of which will not be as happy as the second. Should the subject be of middle-age, this domino fore-tells the speedy arrival of good things and the fact that he or she will never be lonely and uncared for.

Six-blank is, unfortunately, a sign of great trouble - sickness, death, or heavy money losses.

Double-five tells that all achievements will be rewarded with a large amount of success, but inordinate wealth is not prophesied.

Five-four is almost as unfortunate a draw as six-blank. Should a young girl lift it, it means that her future husband will be poor and leave her a widow. Further, he may be of extravagant disposition, in spite of his poverty.

Five-three indicates a tranquil and contented existence. Sufficient money and matrimonial affection of moderate strength, the couple being incapable of passionate devotion.

Five-two conveys a warning that love and marriage are destined to an unhappy termination.

Five-one tells of social popularity, but financial worries and losses.

Five-blank is supposed to demonstrate egotistical and avaricious characteristics, tendencies to swindling and intrigues, also a warning to remain unmarried.

Double-four the person who earns a livelihood by manual labour may regard this domino as a sign of future security and prosperity, but to those whose profession needs mental achievement it is rather disastrous. Troubles and disappointments await.

Four-three indicates matrimony and moderate income.

Four-two proclaims an early marriage and moderate income.

Four-one foretells wealth or many friends.

Four-blank is a sure warning that single life will be the best and happiest. It counsels that any secrets imparted to another will be indiscreetly revealed.

Double-three implies enormous riches.

Three-two foretells prosperity in matrimony, travels, and speculations.

Three-one indicates some danger and unhappiness. The necessity for acting with extreme caution in all matters.

Three-blank warns of domestic unhappiness – such as a quarrel or incompatibility of temperament of husband and wife. The absence of harmony in the home.

Double-two promises average happiness and income.

Two-one is a sign of two marriages, if the individual be a woman; financial failures to a commercial man.

Two-blank implies that the intrigues of unscrupulous people will meet with temporary success. It also denotes poverty, and an indolent husband. The individual will return safely from all journeys undertaken.

Double-one foretells an existence free from money worries; peace and constancy in love and marriage.

Double-blank seems to favour the deeds of unprincipled people, and foretells want of integrity in lover and husband.

Palmistry

Palmistry ranks among the most ancient forms of learning and knowledge. Some palmists justify its study by a text from the Book of Job (Job 37:7—'He sealeth up the hand of every man; that all men may know his work'), but it is known to have been understood in Egypt and, farther back still, among the Hindus.

The art of palmistry takes its place as a serious study in which the deductions are as reliable, if the student can be earnest and intelligent, as those of any other system founded on ordered knowledge.

In this book you will find the art of palmistry reduced to its clearest and simplest form.

The Anatomy of the Hand

The human hand is made up of the metacarpal bones and the phalangeal bones. Between the hand and the bones of the forearm—the radius and ulna—are the eight carpal bones of the wrist, in two rows. Between the carpal bones and the fingers and thumb come the metacarpals. These are similar to the phalangeals, or finger bones, in shape but are longer. They are contained in the muscular envelope of the palm. Jointed to the metacarpals at the knuckles are the bones of the phalanges in three rows, the bones tapering towards the fingertips.

The thumb has only two phalangeal bones and these, like its metacarpal, are shorter than those of the fingers.

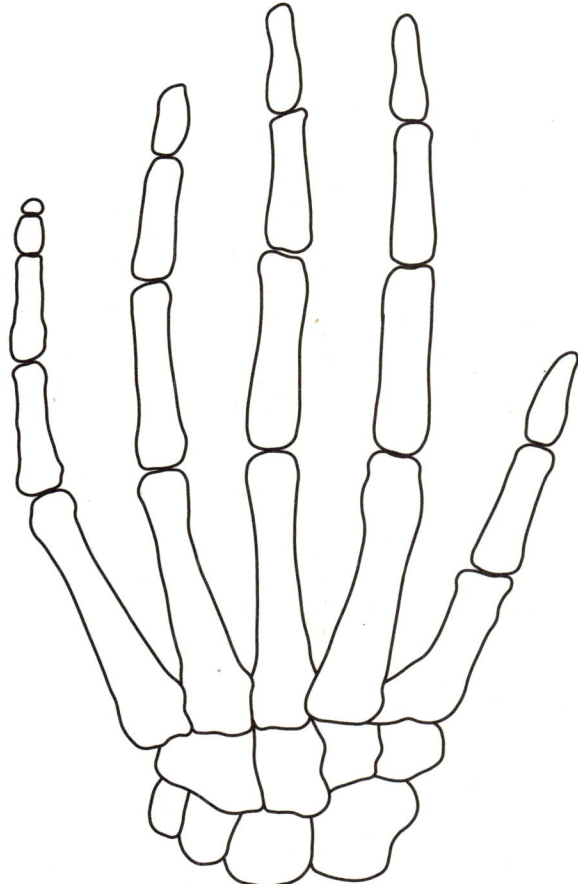

The metacarpal of the thumb is capable of free movement, and it is this characteristic that makes the thumb an 'opposable' digit. Because of this we are able to grasp objects and use our hands in such complex operations as sewing, writing, drawing and working with tools. There are twenty-seven bones in the hand and wrist—eight carpals, five metacarpals and fourteen phalangeal bones.

One result of the great flexibility of the hand is that its palmar surface is thickly padded in between the lines of flexion, or bending, while at these lines the skin is bound down to the tendons that move the digits, and to the deeper layers. This combination of loose and firm surfaces gives the necessary secureness and adaptability to the grasp. It is obvious that if the padding of the palm were loose and free to slip about, a firm grasp would be impossible.

The 'bracelet' lines at the wrist have a similar origin. The monticuli—prominences that we see at the base of the thumb and fingers—are composed of muscle tissue. So too are those on the phalanges. Nature has endowed the hand with the characteristics of flexibility and firmness, and has cushioned the palm against shocks that would otherwise injure its framework.

The Size and Shape of the Hands

Large hands show order, method, obedience and detail.

Small hands show energy, government, ability to rule and executive power.

Medium-sized hands indicate a character with a capacity for turning his or her hand to anything. When the fingers are exactly as long as the palm, they belong to people who are successful in business but not in any highly specialized kind of business. Note that this hand belongs also to the 'Jack-of-all-trades'—the person who does many things capably but none of them exceedingly well.

Hands with palms long in comparison to the length of the fingers, show an ability to make big plans, a quick grasp of things, a dislike of detail.

Hands with the fingers relatively much longer than the palm cannot plan but they can 'finish' everything they do. A person with hands like these will not neglect or overlook the slightest detail. They are the 'slow-but-sure' people.

Wide hands indicate kindness and sympathy—someone who is able to see and consider the other side as well as his or her own point of view.

Narrow hands belong to people who are critical and exacting by nature—those who see one's faults rather than one's good qualities. It is said that the best husbands and wives are not found with this kind of hand, but if the life partner's hand is too short and too wide, fate may draw them together

Hands wide open with the fingers well apart show originality, initiative and courage.

Hands with fingers close together show convention, fear of consequences and cowardice.

White hands show a selfish nature.

Red hands show passionate feeling, anger and energy.

Hands of warmish pink show a warm heart.

Soft hands indicate laziness, which may coexist with distinct and probably unused talent. But, hands that are only moderately soft, or soft on the mounts, may belong to people who work best in short bursts only.

Very hard hands demonstrate energy and the love of work for its own sake. These are people who should ask themselves what it is that they want out of life and then set out to get it, cultivating mental disciplines so that they do not waste their nervous energy too extravagantly.

Square hands show reason, consistency, common sense and accuracy.

Pointed hands show spirituality, idealism.

Note that a hard and very square hand belongs to a person who always has reason on his or her side. He or she is never wrong.

The extremely 'peaky' hand—especially if it lacks 'grip' and feels unreal when it is grasped—belongs to the dreamer, the impractical person. With very pointed fingertips, these hands will have no sense of reality—they will take up and support the wildest notions. Tapering fingertips lack executive power.

There is a third hand, called the spatulate hand, which is the opposite of the pointed hand. It is rare and inclines to be distinctly ugly, with fingers that bulge at the top. This is the useful hand. Its owner is concerned only with material things, but this hand, when not excessively spatulate, belongs to the person of action—the worldly person. Its owner is practical, technically adept and would feel at home working with engines or machinery.

For a person to be an inventor or a really original thinker who can translate his or her thoughts into action, the hand must partake of all these three types, and every one of the fingertips must vary.

The mixed hand is the most difficult to read.

Palmists have over many years, defined seven well-marked types of hands:
The Elemental
The Spatulate or Active
The Conical or Temperamental
The Square or Utilitarian
The Knotty or Philosophic
The Pointed or Idealistic
The Mixed

The Elemental
This hand is the mark of primitive races; it is characteristic of peoples, such as the Laplanders, who inhabit Polar regions, and was also a feature of the Tartar and Slav

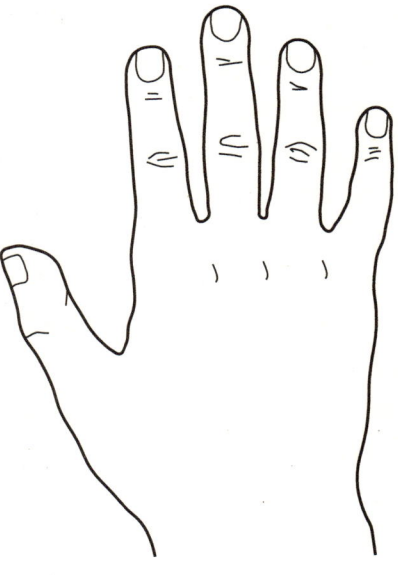

races. The palm is large, and the fingers short and thick. It is intrinsically the hand of the peasant or the serf of times long past, it is seen in all lands among those who for generations have come from the stock that furnishes the 'hewers of wood and drawers of water'. These people have, in the course of centuries, evolved as a type who have adapted to making a living by hard and rough labour; their acquisitive and self-preservative faculties have developed to predominance.

What significance is to be attached to the possession of an elemental hand in our subject? It depends, of course, on the degree of relation to the archetype, for the pure elemental is uncommon outside those regions that have been mentioned.

Superstitious, narrow-mined and unintellectual, this type has nevertheless produced, on occasion, great leaders—in religious persecutions and in the rare and dreadful peasant risings in European history.

The Spatulate or Active
This hand is large and broad, with blunt, thick fingers, broad at the tips. The digits are long. It is the mark of someone of action rather than a great thinker, of the tireless, restless agitator who seeks to improve the lot of others by his or her endeavours and adventure,of the

bold and daring navigator of Polar seas, or of the courageous pioneer.

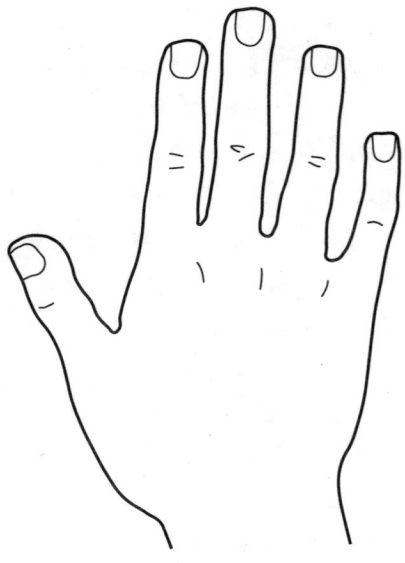

People with the spatulate hand have certainly played their part in history, linking the Atlantic and the Pacific by railway, in cutting canals such as the Suez and the Panama, in opening up air routes across continents and oceans. They are generally intolerant of convention, and are highly original in thought and action. Women of the spatulate type are endowed with a large measure of intuition.

In games and athletics they may excel, and usually they are musical. Some of the greatest painters of all time have belonged to the spatulate type. In general, this hand denotes the executive rather than the administrator. Rulers of this group have made history by their failures rather than by their achievements.

The Conical or Temperamental

This type of hand marks the emotional or temperamental subject—impetuous, impulsive and exuberant. The aesthetic perception is strongly developed, and beauty in all forms and guises appeals strongly to this person. Although scarcely artistic in the real sense of the term, he or she is sensitive to the emotional stimulus of music and pictures. A somewhat unstable nature is indicated—

the temperament being coloured by varying moods which never endure long. Although generally cheerful and optimistic, this person is, however, easily depressed by any misfortune or by lack of success in trivial enterprises, and the mood of satisfaction may change suddenly to one of black despair.

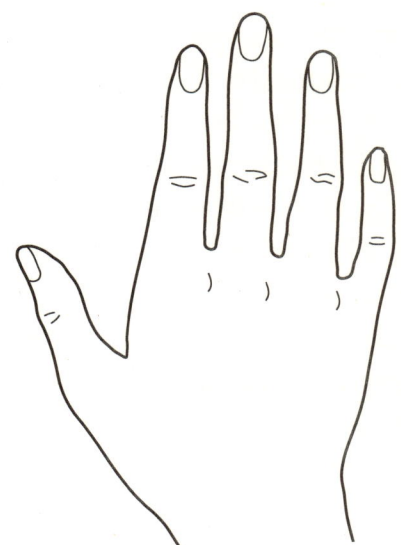

The content of his or her mind is coloured by the conversation of any and every person he or she meets. Lacking skill in constructive thought, this type reflects the moods and opinions of those stronger surrounding personalities.

The wife or husband of this type is a somewhat difficult person. He or she does not easily tolerate discipline, dislikes mundane routine, and craves for pleasure and excitement—for something new or different. Whilst hot-tempered, this person is soon repentant after an outburst of passion, and so avoids making enemies.

The Square or Utilitarian

This type of hand denotes the methodical, matter-of-fact individual, who is a steady, law-abiding member of society. Though this person may not rise to great heights in intellectual matters, he or she is a plodder who very often reaps rewards as a result of industry and perseverance. In contrast to the owner of a spatulate hand, the utilitarian hand generally represents a conservative outlook and a sturdy support of the existing order of things—in religion, in politics and in business. He or she often responds to change with immediate and intense opposition.

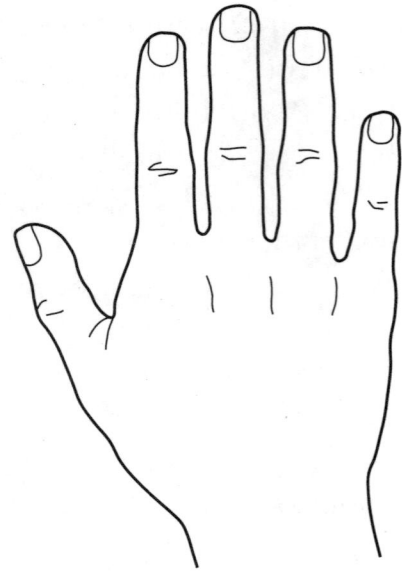

A very valuable member of the community, he or she appears as the successful lawyer, politician or teacher who makes progress as much through self restraint as through good deeds. The owner of a utilitarian hand is a good soldier but a poor leader, because the utilitarian type is nonplussed when an opponent disregards the 'rules' or does something contrary to his or her own experience.

The man of this group makes a good match for a woman who is not passionately demanding. In matrimony, he is apt to take things too much for granted, frequently forgetting that his partner expects material, physical and emotional evidence of his love.

The Knotty or Philosophic

This hand is noticeable for its bluntly conical fingertips, its large joints and its broad third phalanges. It denotes a materialistic type of mind; logical, methodical and systematic. This is the hand of the seeker of life's truths.

Such a person is inclined to be reserved and to appear

'standoffish.' This is quite undeserved; the reserve arises merely from a profound knowledge of and an interest in matters that only a few people will care to talk about. In the absence of people with similar interests, the philosophic appears aloof; but place him *en rapport* with a kindred spirit and his or her reserve vanishes. In the young person this temperament in-

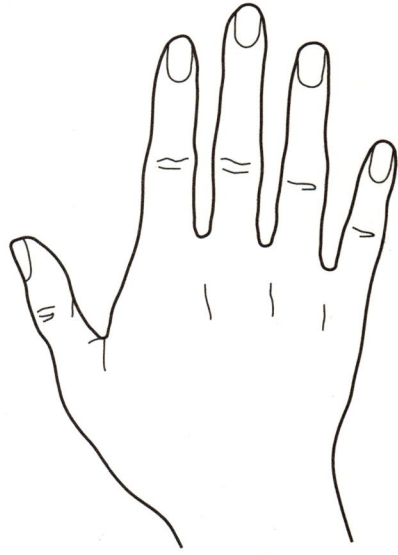

evitably leads to a somewhat introspective tendency, and the subject is, generally, not a 'good mixer'.

A hard worker, the philosophic is honest with him or herself as well as with others—philosophic types have few delusions about themselves, though they will always back their own opinions when they eventually arrive at them. They endeavour to keep an open mind during investigation or analysis of evidence. Although the philosophic may not be ideal as a choice of partner, he or she is generally a good parent, though just and stern. He or she may be sceptical about religion, but, nevertheless, might maintain a firm commitment to some creed.

The Pointed or Idealistic

This hand marks the possessor as one who worships at the shrine of beauty—not material beauty so much as beauty of the mind, though the artistic perception is usually well developed and the subject appreciates true beauty in everything. As a rule, the idealistic type is rather impractical in mundane matters, and has little idea of thrift or provision for future wants—like the grasshopper in the fable, who sings during the sunny hours, but may starve in the winter of life.

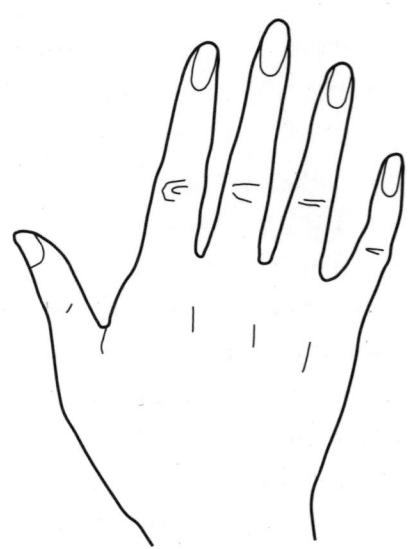

Gifted with a vivid and creative imagination, people of this type love verse and literature; frequently they write, paint or compose. A marriage of two such persons is usually an ideally happy one, though the parties may have to suffer poverty. On the other hand, should the similarity of temperament be merely superficial, then intense unhappiness may result. Being naturally fickle and inconstant, idealistic types are in need of a very strong bond of love to hold them to their life partners.

This type finds much comfort in religious practices and good works. He or she worships wholeheartedly, and feels that beautiful music, pictures, lights etc, fit in best with his or her idea of devotion. The less aesthetic side of religion holds less attraction for the idealistic type— theirs is not the stuff of which martyrs are made. We take an extreme case, of course—the pointed type is rare, and in its completeness is rarer still.

The Mixed

This hand is one that cannot be readily classified in any of the other six groups, for it contains characteristics of some of all of them. Thus, the palm may be large and the fingers long, thick at the lower phalange and then tapering. It thus has points of the idealistic type and others that associate it more with the utilitarian. In another subject we may observe characteristics of both the active and philosophic types of hand. The rule of interpretation is to give value to the most important features. If these are contradictory an average is indicated.

Generally, a mixed hand indicates an adaptable temperament and some versatility. The latter quality may be so much in evidence that the subject turns out to be a 'Jack-of-all-trades' and fails to make a success of his or her life in consequence. Many brilliant engineers, inventors and research workers have belonged to this type, spending their life in pursuit of new technologies and developments. But, when they have solved their problems they are not materially better off—though the world has profited from their discoveries.

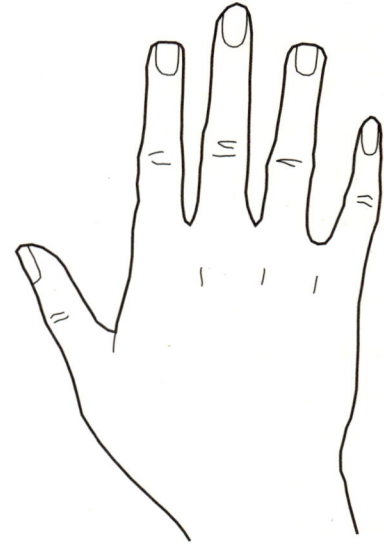

The attributes indicated in a mixed hand are those of the types to which it is nearest in form. There are many varieties, and each must be analysed on its merits.

The Female Hand

Though the female hand, as well as the male, is classified in the seven types identified, the distinguishing features are not so strongly marked. A woman's hands are softer, smoother and more modelled, but the characteristics which have been highlighted can be identified.

The elemental hand is rare in the gentler sex, and the spatulate and knotty types are less conspicuous than in the male. When any one of these three is found with strongly marked features, the attributes are present in large measure. As to the temperamental and idealistic, the interpreter may here fall into the error of over-valuation, for in many women the hand has something of these features without, however, belonging really to either type. The square or utilitarian type is more easily recognized; and the mixed type, too, can usually be distinguished.

The Fingers and the Mounts

The first or index finger is the finger of Jupiter.

The second or middle finger is the finger of Saturn.

The third or wedding-ring finger is the finger of Apollo.

The fourth or little finger is the finger of Mercury.

The natural bend of the fingers is important, and the palmist should be quick to notice its natural attitude before examining the interior of the hand.

Some fingers are distinguished by their independent, prominent position over the rest. When the tips are inclined to curl to the palm, a plodding, determined nature is indicated; one that does not easily relinquish a set aim or purpose because of obstacles.

A wide space between Jupiter and Saturn shows un-

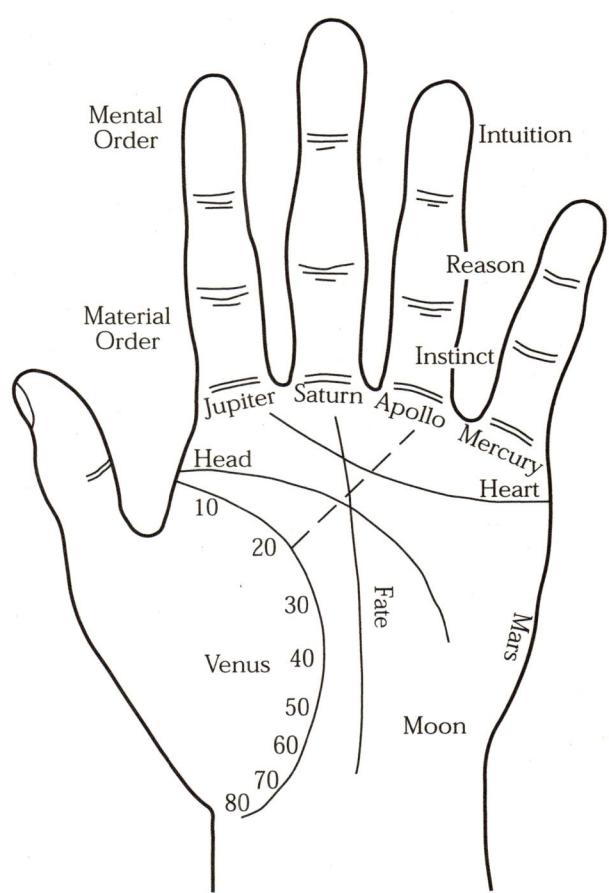

conventionality, and originality of thought and outlook.

When the Jupiter finger is upright and straight, and of normal length, a just, candid nature is revealed. Should its position be in advance of the other fingers, a respect for authority is indicated. If it falls slightly behind, this indicates dependency on others and a reluctance to take the initiative and the burden of responsibility. If the finger is short this denotes ingratitude and no enthusiasm. If it is pointed it is an indication of tact, comprehension, and sympathy. A square finger is a sign of integrity, but also some one who may be thoughtlessly frank in expressing opinions.

The generous and broad phalanges of Saturn show gravity, depth of character, and a sense of proportion. A short Saturn signifies imprudence and an inclination to act on impulse and behave rashly— spatulate implies energy, and square indicates cool, clear-headed, thought before action and absence of hasty judgements.

If the finger of Apollo is well-developed this shows artistic tendencies. If its position is slightly forward, the talent lies in painting, drawing, or sculpture. A pointed finger is a sign that the artistic ability is greater than the practical. A spatulate shape shows a sense of the beautiful in form and colour, and possession of dramatic powers.

Mercury, set lower than the other fingers, reveals the fact that many adverse circumstances have been battled with. A pointed finger of Mercury indicates tact, discrimination and intuition. If it is square it shows a love of scientific pursuits and good reasoning powers.

The mounts under each bear the same names as the fingers above them. Thus we have the Mounts of Jupiter, Saturn, Apollo and Mercury.

The mount at the base of the thumb is the Mount of Venus, and that opposite to it on the fleshy outer base of the hand, is the Mount of Luna or of the moon. There are, in addition, two Mounts of Mars situated respectively above the Mount of Venus and below the Mount of Jupiter; this is Mars Positive. On the outer side of the hand, above the Mount of Luna and below that of the Mount of Mercury is situated Mars Negative.

As the fingers and their supporting mounts represent

the same qualities, it is easier to simultaneously learn what the fingers and mounts stand for. However, note that the finger in excess (i.e. exceptionally long or large) stands for the nobler overdevelopment of the qualities, and the mounts in excess stand for their more fatalistic or baser over-expression. The hand is like the head in this respect. In the top part we read of the intellectual qualities, and at the base of the animal instincts.

Fingers that are weak or small and mounts that are quite flat, show absence of the qualities represented. Mounts that seem to be almost hollow—though this *may* be due to the very high development of the 'neighbouring' Mount—indicate the qualities opposite to those for which the fingers stand.

Remember that in palmistry, as in most everything else, *excess* is not a good thing. In real life the excess of any virtue may prove a vice! The wise ever seek to direct their actions in line with:

'. . .the happy mean,

A Vice at each side and the Virtue between.'

Thus, the excess of prudence is the vice of miserliness on one side, and its absence is prodigality on the other.

Jupiter

Jupiter stands for veneration, worship, religion. A very dominant first finger indicates the hands of great religious leaders and all those whose sense of honour is extremely high. With the mount big and out of proportion, then religious mania or enthusiasm run wild. If the mount is hard, fanaticism is indicated—if it is soft and high then the subject is said to be of sympathetic nature but with strange beliefs.

Saturn

Saturn stands for knowledge, thought, occultism, super-stition. This second mount, if unusually high, will de-note fatalism, melancholy and esoteric knowledge. The subject will say— 'I cannot do or undo. What must be, will be.'

When the second finger is big and square, this indi-cates a thoughtful but not a practical person—a pointed finger is a sign of unbalanced thought.

When Saturn's Mount is flat, there is a total lack of imagination; and people without imagination are apt to be cruel. But this mount may appear flat, because of the height of Apollo which denotes joyousness, as distinct from the sadness of Saturn.

Apollo

Apollo signifies art, beauty, wealth and joy in living.

This mount is highly developed in all artists who have an inborn love of colour and of beauty. But if the hand is soft, there may be an over-strong enjoyment of pleas-ure through the senses. If the Mount of Apollo is flat it illustrates a nature that detests joy and almost seems to dislike beauty and dread happiness.

A long thin finger of Apollo indicates a love of colour, and if the thumb is strong there will be capacity to ex-press this in some form of art.

Mercury

Mercury denotes persuasive speech, business and worldly shrewdness. If the mount is very high and the finger pointed, it indicates a person who is perhaps 'too clever' or even tricky, especially if Jupiter is poor. A crooked little finger indicates a thief, one who steals not because he needs to steal, but because he likes to do so. The Mount of Mercury, if very flat, shows an individual with no foresight and the inability to seize a chance when it presents itself. Mercury's finger, if square at the top, shows one who can both buy and sell to advantage.

So much for the Mounts that distinctly belong to the fingers.

The Thumb

The possession of a thumb, a digit that can be placed in opposition to the fingers, differentiates man from all the animals except certain apes and monkeys. It is a most valuable addition, for man could never have developed without it. The ability to make and use crude and rough tools enabled our primitive ancestors to set out on the evolutionary path that has led to our civilization of to-day. From rough tools man could fashion finer and more efficient ones—first of flint, then of bronze and iron—and utilize them to build and construct. No wonder the thumb is such a valuable index to character and temperament.

The characteristics of the thumb, in general, are those of the type of hand to which it belongs; but there are certain special features of the thumb that are worthy of attention. First of all, let us mention the rare case where the thumb is absent or is very small—this is perhaps a sign denoting degeneration to a primitive type. Ordinarily the thumb, when placed close to the index-finger, reaches to the joint or just below it. If it does not reach this joint it is a short thumb. If it goes beyond the joint the thumb is said to be long.

The thumb has only two phalanges—the first or top-most one is associated with willpower and executive ability, and the second with logical perception and reasoning powers. The size of the first phalange is important in reading the hand, for if the phalange is large it denotes that other tendencies indicated by the fingers and other parts of the hand are likely to be effective. If the contrary is the case, tendencies remain dormant unless there is enough willpower to ensure that these gifts can be actively employed.

The thumb, then, is a real index to character. By the proportionate size of the two phalanges it denotes whether will or reason will have the upper hand in guiding the actions of the subject; if both phalanges are much the same in size, the individual will employ both these mental faculties equally in determining his way of life. At the base of the thumb is the mount of Venus, indicating the love propensity. If well developed, it shows that the subject is swayed by his heart a good deal in coming to decisions. Palmists sometimes describe the part of the thumb beneath the mount as the third phalange.

If the thumb lies close to the fingers we can say that the owner is careful with money and not too generous. A looser thumb, standing away from the hand, denotes a freer, more open nature. Then, too, we can note whether the thumb is supple at the top joint, or stiff and unyielding. In the former case we may say the subject is broad-minded, generous, tolerant and good-humoured; moreover, he can readily adapt himself to different circumstances. In the man with the stiff-jointed thumb we should expect qualities that are almost the opposite of those just mentioned—caution, reserve, an obstinate adherence to somewhat narrow views of life and morals, and a determination to obtain what are regarded as rights. With this sign should be considered the relative sizes of the first and second phalange.

It is useful to have some standard by which to measure the relative size of the two phalanges of the thumb. Various proportions have been suggested as the normal one; it may be taken that the first or end phalange should be nearly half the length of the thumb, the second being slightly longer. In the left hand it is likely that the phalanges will show quite a different proportional size, when examining a left-handed subject the left hand should be taken as the representative one.

Sometimes the thumb is broadened and 'clubbed' at the tip, which is full and plump. This denotes a passionate, hot-tempered individual, swayed excessively by his emotions and easily roused to intense anger.

More about the Fingers

The fingers, as you will see, are divided by two knuckles or 'knots' into three divisions.

The top space, which includes the tips with the nails at the back, is the first phalange, devoted to will, as is the top of the thumb. If this is long, fine, or pointed, there is also imagination—length indicates the will to express artistic imagination. If thick, an obstinate will. If thick and long, a strong, dominating will. But the thumb ought not to be set low on the hand if the talent is original or creative.

The middle or second phalange belongs to reason. If this is long, then the person thinks things out and, if the hand is fairly square and capable-looking, they are able to plan ahead. Good organizers have a strong second phalange. A short space stands for those who have no use for reason. But with a clever hand, their intuition will serve them well. They will 'get there' if they trust their own perceptions, and act on their first impressions.

The third phalange, if thick and long, belongs to people of a passionate nature. But this phalange of the fingers shows the nobler aspect of the animal nature, just as that at the very base of the hand under Venus, coming as it does in the lowest part of the hand, expresses the physical side.

As for the knots that divide the phalanges, the upper knot dividing the first from the second phalange is the knot of philosophy. Large and well developed, it shows a love of accurate thinking, of exact knowledge. If small, it indicates those who are not at all philosophical; those whose acts are not ruled by their heads. Impetuous people generally have poor knots of philosophy.

The lower knot, which divides the second from the third phalange, is the knot of order. It belongs to great talkers. These are also good talkers, for we generally do well in what we enjoy doing most. People who talk well must have well developed sense of order, though they are seldom credited with this. Yet, without it, how could they find the right word and set it in the right place at the right moment?

In a long and narrow hand, a knot that is prominent will show a contradictory, contentious, quarrelsome person. But in a clever, short hand that is wide, indicating kindness, it means a love of debate, a talent for 'stating a case' and ability to prove things. With a crooked little finger, you might get a clever liar, if this knot is strong. But where there is sympathy (a wide hand), and a thumb set low (talent), and good head and heart lines, these talkers generally turn their charming talent to their own advantage.

The Fingernails

The nails are developed from skin tissues, and so partake of the intimate nature of the flesh. It is remarkable that in people of mixed blood the nails may denote this fact. Even when the blood has been thinned down for a number of generations, the nails may still show signs of ancestry. Then, too, the nails show signs of disease, for example, becoming curved inwards in consumption or tuberculosis. Clubbed fingers are another symptom of this disorder. It is common knowledge that in some cases of poisoning the harmful substance may show its presence when the nails are subjected to chemical examination.

Long nails denote a calm, phlegmatic temperament— short ones suggest a more impetuous nature. When the finger nails are well formed, with good crescents and a rounded, shapely base, we may expect an equable nature and sound judgement. A broad and curved top, associated with the last-named characteristics, denotes an open, generous and frank mind. Narrow, elongated nails are found on people of somewhat delicate constitution, and are often pale and bloodless or even bluish in colour. When unaccompanied by any signs of ill health, the long and moderately narrow nail suggests a refined and idealistic or psychic type of individual. Nails with a spatulate end, especially when broad in proportion to their length, denote pugnacity. When the nails show a reddish colouring, this attribute is strengthened.

In general, the nails should be pinkish to reddish in

hue, and not pale or bluish. Ridged or grooved nails suggest a naturally nervous temperament, though this sign may denote nothing more than an alert and sensitive mind. Any irregularities in the shape, form, or colouring of the nails are signs of health defects. Blueness that persists is a sign of some defect of the circulatory system. The nails are of secondary importance to the fingers as an index to character, though they may afford useful indications to health and temperament.

The Lines of the Hand

The Line of Life (A) runs around the base of the Mount of Venus.

The Line of Head (B) runs across the centre of the hand, starting under Jupiter.

The Line of Heart (C) runs across the upper part of the palm directly under the mounts.

The Line of Fate (D) (or Line of Destiny) is one of the two most important lines on the hand, the other being the Line of Life. It runs from low down on the hand straight through the centre, up towards the finger of Saturn.

The Line of Fortune (E) (or the Line of Apollo or the Sun) also runs up the hand towards the finger of Apollo, or the ring finger.

The Line of Intuition (F) is rare in its perfect form. It is a semicircle, a longish semicircle or oval line running round or partly round the Mount of Luna.

The Girdle of Venus (G) is rare. When found, it is above the Heart Line, a small half-circular mark around or partly around the two middle Mounts of Jupiter and Saturn.

The Line of Mars (H) is a smaller half-circle sometimes found within the Line of Life.

The Line of Health (J) (or the Line of Mercury) on which business affairs is also read, is a third line running up the hand, but somewhat transversely, towards the finger of Mercury.

Finally come the Bracelets, three lines (or two or only one in some cases), that run halfway around the wrists, under the front of the hand.

It will be observed that the line of life, line of head

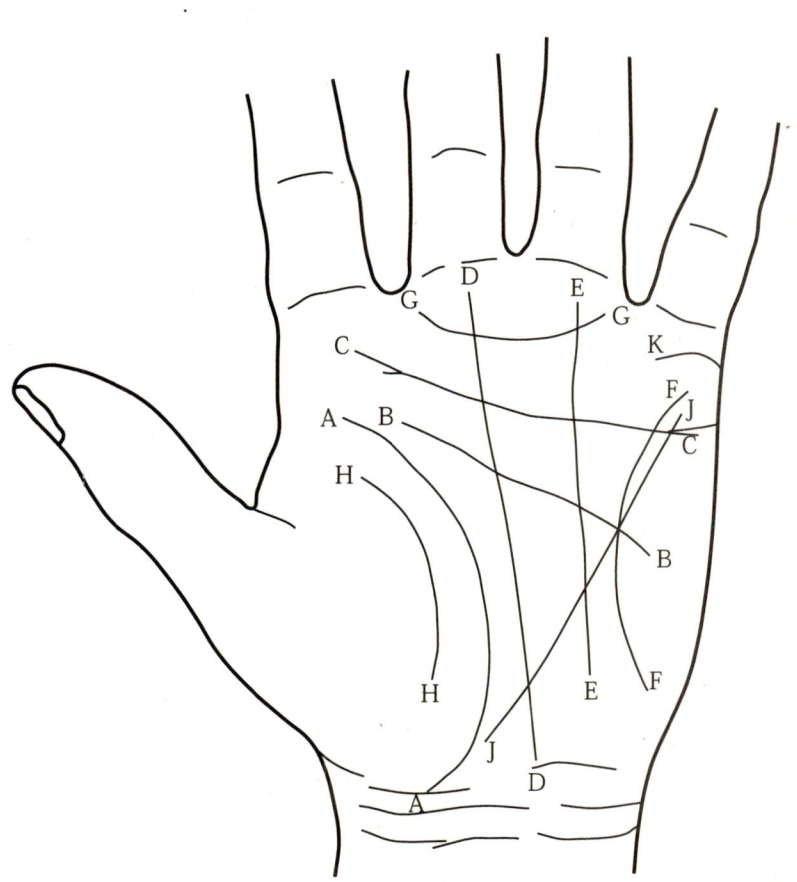

and line of health between them form a triangle, which is called the Great Triangle. Note also that the line of Sun, line of destiny, line of head and line of heart form the Quadrangle at their intersection.

Age and Time Calculations

Time is calculated on these lines of the hands, as you will see by looking at the diagram. We have one hundred years to be read on the Line of Life at its fullest and longest, that is, when it actually goes round and almost behind the thumb base. The age at which certain events, represented by crosses, squares, triangles, and other marks will happen, can be calculated fairly accurately if the palmist will remember:

- the middle of the Line of Life stands for the fiftieth year
- the centre of the Head Line represents the age of thirty-five
- where the Line of Fate touches the Head Line at its centre is this same important age of thirty-five
- the age of thirty-five is read on the Line of Heart under the centre of the finger of Apollo. Palmistry gives the larger half of Heart events, to the years before thirty-five.

In real life, as in palmistry, we 'count time by heart beats' and not by hours or years. It is a mistake to think that all hours—or years—are exactly the same length.

Doubtless the most interesting marks to be found among the minor lines of the hand, which indicate voyages, change of environment, talents and ambitions, are those that concern the attachments, love affairs, and future marriage of the subject.

These are the influence lines, which may be discerned running from Mount Luna to the line of Fate, from Mount Venus to the Line of Life, and on the Mount of Mercury. Their depth, length, and clarity depend upon the enduring nature of the sentiment involved. When crossed, barred, or cut, they demonstrate the fact that difficulties and opposition from parents, friends, or relatives are to be encountered, or it may be that the influence was merely a fleeting infatuation.

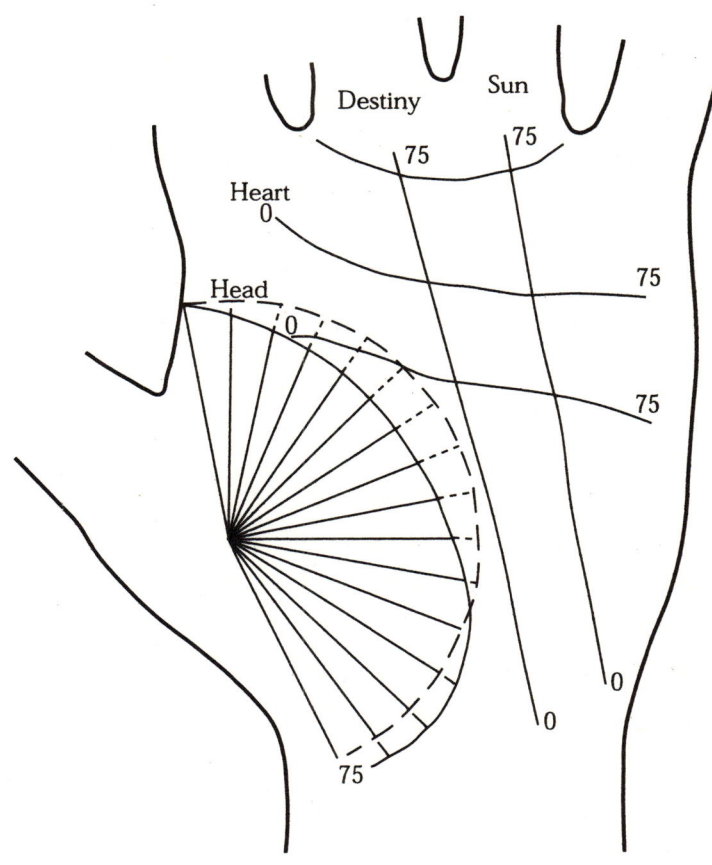

These signs should be compared with the age calculated upon the fate line—it will then be discovered whether the influence lines are of the past, present, or future. Only constant practice and experience can aid the reader to a correct estimate of the period of these happenings.

How to Read the Lines

Date Lines

The chronology used in palmistry is based upon a division of certain of the lines into year-periods. The Line of Heart, Line of Head, Line of Destiny, Line of Sun and Line of Life are those chiefly used for determining ages or dates. The span of man's life can be taken at 75 years for the purpose of these readings, and the lines are graduated accordingly. The Line of Life reads downwards, and the Lines of Destiny and the Sun are read upwards. The Lines of Heart and Head are read from their origin at the thumb side of the palm.

These lines can be divided into four-, six- or seven-year intervals, or as in this text, a five-year interval.

The Line of Life

The Line of Life, long, even and clear, represents a long and healthy life. If broken in one hand, this life line tells of a serious illness. If completely broken in both hands, then life may end at that age. However, the life line may grow again and the broken lines join together, especially if more than five years lie between the date at which the hand is read and the time when the life lines in both hands end. Thus, no serious palmist would pretend to be able to tell the age at which death occurs.

Note that this Life Line, if chained, tells of delicacy and illness, caused by anxiety, unhappiness, or worry. If the line is red, there is a tendency to fevers. If it is purple, it shows a tendency to inherited illnesses. One often sees a faint purplish shade on part of the Line of Life of one hand. If in the left hand only, this shows actual illness has been avoided.

Both hands must be read, and when the Life Line shows a series of fine crosses set closely together, this indicates the occurrence of neuralgic pains and aches at the time indicated. If these are repeated on the Line of Head, then this indicates pain of a more serious nature, occurring in the head. This Life Line, pale or thin, tells of poor health generally during those years. But the smaller Line of Mars inside the Life Line promises survival, and corrects or modifies indications of poor health or of short life.

Branches upwards from the Line of Life tell of honours or successes that are purely fortuitous. Thus, if an individual achieves high office his palm will show a branch upwards from the Line of Fate. This individual's partner, for whom this honour is fortuitous, might show a branch on the Life Line.

The Line of Head

When this line is long there is talent and a naturally good memory. But if it is too closely linked up with the beginning of the Line of Life (thus making only one line under the Mount of Jupiter) there is a marked lack of self-confidence. If they continue as one for over half an inch, then this self-distrust will greatly hamper and delay success, however talented the subject is.

The Line of Head starting slightly apart from the Life Line gives a steady self-confidence. But if the space between is very wide (7mm is very wide here) this shows rash impulsiveness; review and re-evaluation will always be advisable for these people.

The Head Line, if short, shows impulse, prejudice, a lack of reasoning power and a tendency to act first and think afterwards. The Line of Head when straight and long shows thrift and economy (with no imagination, if very straight). Long, and tending slightly downwards at the end shows sympathy and an ability to see the viewpoint of other people. If drooping low down to the base of the hand, the subject has too much imagination. If apparent in both hands, along with a weak thumb, then it may indicate mental weakness.

If the Line of Head is divided into a large fork at the end, one branch of which goes straight across the hand and the other turns down on to the Mount of Luna or even towards the wrist, this shows that life has two sides—the practical side, which will be efficiently conducted, and a vivid and very real life of the imagination. The hands of novelists typically show this handsome forking on the Head Lines.

If the Head Line is blurred this indicates an illness in which there has been delirium. If it is broken in one hand, the subject may commit a serious error of judgement. A line broken in both hands, is a warning that the subject may suffer an accident where his or her head is injured in some way.

The Line of Heart
When this is clear and long, it gives a happy life, rich in

affection. But if it misses the Mount of Jupiter, rising from up between that mount and the next one, the Mount of Saturn, there is coldness as regards love with a tormenting capacity for jealousy. If this is apparent on one hand only, this tendency is kept under control admirably. Hands in which the Heart Line misses Jupiter do not find happiness in love. When it starts under Saturn there is coldness and a lack of feeling.

A short Heart Line denotes selfishness in love, where flirting takes the place of affection and may be mistaken for it. A series of very small crosses on the Heart Line indicates suffering through the unworthiness of those loved.

A broken Heart Line shows a broken engagement or similar emotional trauma. Breaks under the Mount of Jupiter indicate the cause was honour; under Saturn, this indicates that the cause was a fatality, perhaps death; under Apollo, pride with some mystery. The subject does not know *why* the break came, and is too proud to find out. Under Mercury, the broken Heart Line means that the person who was loved was thoroughly unworthy.

The Girdle of Venus

The Girdle of Venus used to be read as a sign of an evil life. Now, however, it is more correctly taken to mean the likelihood of some great unhappiness in relation to an emotional attachment. Its ugly aspect will have passed over by the time the subject reaches his or her thirty-fifth year.

If a man has this half-ring, he will be well advised not to marry until that age has passed, nor indeed to form any important partnerships. If a married woman is seen to have this girdle, the wise palmist will tell her to 'sit tight'. She will surely get on better with her unsatisfactory life partner *after* she has turned thirty-five. This ill-omened mark also tells of sudden death touching the life. The Girdle of Venus always tells of a catastrophe that has occurred in the earlier part of the life

The Line of Fate
This may start from four places:
- From the Bracelets—this indicates an uncommon destiny, that may mean great happiness or misery, according to the way in which the life is lived. However, the circumstances are, as a rule, out of the subject's choice with this 'start' of the Fate Line.
- From the Line of Life—this shows a good life with good chances. The subject makes his own way in life.
- From the Mount of the Moon—fate is made by marriage or entirely through the decisions or doings of other people.
- From the middle of the hand—a hard life, troubled and hampered by poverty or cruel circumstances.

But the Line of Fate that ends high up in the hand, even though it starts over high up, *does* spell success at the end. Breaks in this line are not negative, they represent changes. If the line goes on straight and clear, these may be good changes. Branches towards the Moon tell of travels; towards Jupiter, of honours and dignities earned.

Branches that rise from the outer side and touch the Fate Line denote affairs of the heart. Those that are clear and touch the fate lines of both hands indicate marriage at the age where they touch. A good cross on Jupiter ought to confirm this indication.

Sometimes the Fate Line, after starting well and low down in the hand, disappears for some years and then reappears. This means that the life is uneventful during those years. The Money Line also disappears sometimes. Widowhood, represented by a line from the Fate Line touching the Heart Line and ending in a cross, often brings out both the Fate Line and the Money Line again, later on in life. This only if the widow obtains control of money because of her bereavement.

Absence of the Fate Line does not mean anxiety. It shows that the person is only 'vegetating' when there is no Fate Line. Small lines across the Fate Line are troubles.

The Line of Fortune

This tells of money matters. When it drops for some time it has the same meaning as the fading of the Fate Line. This line, chained or blurred, tells of actual struggling, of 'hard times' due to the absence of money or to our expenditures being more than our income.

A long clear line going right up to the Mount of Apollo tells of riches, a successful life as regards financial fortune. If it bites into the finger, then there is a kind of 'glorious' fortune; great inheritance or a fortune received through some kind of 'luck'.

The Line of Business and of Health

This shows the career, if indeed there is one. This line, standing out prominently and going straight up to the Mount of Mercury, speaks of a successful career. Branches jutting out signify tests, adventures and experiences in new lines of work. If these last while the original line fades out, then this indicates that there will be a clear change of occupation. If forked at the top, this line shows there is great practical ability in the individual. If it is thick, this indicates a delicate old age; if it is red and thin, this shows feverish tendencies. Beware of excitement if this line looks 'angry'.

The Line of Intuition

The Line of Intuition gives great sympathy, instinctive cleverness, intuitive judgement. Perfectly formed, this line belongs to the 'Seer', the clairvoyant. Being on the Mount of the Moon, it implies sadness, even unhappiness:

'For foresight is a melancholy gift
Which bares the bald and speeds the all-tooswift.'

The Bracelets

These tell of successful life, money, and gains in general. It is said that each of these lines, if it is clear and deep (but not too wide) indicates some thirty years of joyful living. But if one of the lines or some part of any of them is chained, there is a fight against poverty and difficult circumstances during that period of thirty years, or the part of them that is chained.

The Bracelets are read as beginning from the end under the thumb. The one nearest the hand stands for the first 30 years of life; the centre line for the period between 30 and 60 years. These are years of effort and struggle in any life that is lived in an honourable way. The lowest line represents the period between 60 and 90 years. You can understand why few hands have these three lines clear and unbroken!

Branches on any age of the lines tell of legacies. The year, in which the legacy or the various legacies are received can be accurately computed by means of the age instructions already given.

The Triangle

Note that the lines of Head, Life and Fate should form a well-defined triangle under the two middle fingers. If this triangle is weak at the junction of any two of the three lines, look for failure or disappointment affecting the destiny of the subject in connection with the qualities represented by those two lines.

Thus, if the triangle is cramped owing to the Head Line being joined to the Life Line, then a lack of self-confidence hinders success. If the Head Line spoils the triangle, owing to its going far down on the Mount of Luna instead of straight across the middle of the hand, a too active imagination is the enemy. With warm affections, a too imaginative Head Line spells jealousy!

If the Life Line stops short and so spoils the triangle, life is cut short and success hindered by this. The Fate Line weak or poor or absent in the early part of life sometimes spoils the shape of the triangle. In this case, early hardships, struggles, lack of friends, etc, may cause failure.

The Plain of Mars

The Plain of Mars is the space between the two mounts of that name. It lies between the lines of the Heart and of the Head, and should be clear and wide. That is, the Heart Line should not drop into it nor the Head Line rise up on to it. I fit is hollow, then this plain is said to show early exile from home. If this plain is clear and well defined in the left hand, it indicates skill in chess and in strategy—in the right hand, with other indications of courage, bravery with skill.

Reading Both Hands

Note that the left hand stands for the natural and the *fated* things, the right hand for what we do with them. The right hand is the hand of *free will*. If one hand is distinctly 'bad', showing a poor Fate Line, crossed and broken, or a badly broken Line of Fortune, it is better for this to be the left hand, because the right hand *may* show improvement. In this case, there will have been a brave fight and the fighter has made things better than they were originally.

If the left hand is 'good' and the right one 'bad', then this says that good health has been wasted, money prospects lost sight of, and hopeful chances thrown away. It is important never to 'tell' anything really important until you have found it to be so in both hands. Now let us study the small signs and symbols on the lines and the mounts.

Crosses

Crosses are bad when they are badly formed. A well-formed cross on Jupiter's Mount stands for a good marriage. On Saturn's Mount, ill-luck. When Saturn's Line (the Line of Fate) goes up into the actual finger, ending there with a cross, there is a great and uncommon destiny, with tragedy at the ending.

A cross on the Line of Fate is always an obstacle, a 'check' to the fate.

A cross lying near it, but not on it, is an obstacle to a life near. Note that the Line of Fate that stops short in the middle of the hand indicates failure, however well it starts up.

A cross on Apollo's Mount, means ill-luck connected with art or literature. On the Mount of Mercury, it shows a loss of money or ill-gotten gains. On the Line of Intuition it shows delusions, on the Line of Life, it indicates an illness. A cross beside the Line of Life, points to illness or trouble to some life near. A cross in the Plain of Mars (in middle of the palm under Saturn) signifies love of the Occult, attraction to magic, etc.

Stars

Stars are fatalities. One on the Mount of Jupiter indicates honours. On Mount of Saturn, you find the signs of danger of death by violence. On the Mount of Apollo, it indicates unhappy riches. On the Mount of Mercury, theft or dishonour may be indicated. A star in the Plain of Mars, that is, between the two Mounts of Mars, signifies military glory. On the Mount of Luna, may be indicative of danger of drowning. A star low on the Head Line, points to insanity in the family—high up on the Head Line, it is a signal of danger of loss of sight. A star on Line of Fortune signifies catastrophe.

Squares

Squares are good. They add force and strength to the qualities indicated by the mounts where they appear. But a Square on the inside of the Line of Life, represents imprisonment or seclusion of some kind. Note the age at which the Square touches the Life Line.

Triangles

Triangles indicate some special talent or aptitude—on Jupiter, for diplomacy, on Saturn, for magic, on Apollo, for art or literature, on Mercury, for success (money success) in politics. A triangle on the Mount of Venus tells of a prudent marriage. Triangles also represent deliverance from danger and misfortune.

Dots

Dots are sometimes of good *or* evil omen. White dots on the Heart Line tell of success in love. Red dots on Heart Line, point to emotional love affairs. Dark dots on Head Line indicate eye trouble. White dots on Head Line, success in invention, according to which Mount they appear under.

Islands

Islands that are made by the line dividing and then joining up again about half an inch further on are always bad. On the Life Line, they tell of hereditary illness. On the Heart Line, an unworthy attachment is indicated. On the Health Line they tell of the same illness as on the Life Line, but this, though serious, is not fatal.

Grills

Grills or crossed lines always show obstacles. They take from the good effects of the qualities indicated by the Mounts, just as Squares add to these qualities. A Grill on Jupiter tells of tyranny and superstition. On Saturn it denotes misfortune. On Apollo a grill indicates folly, vanity and extravagance. On Mercury it is a sign of hypocrisy, lying and theft. A Grill on Mars tells of sudden death and on Luna it signifies anxiety, discontent, sadness.

Marriage

Marriage is indicated by a large cross on the Mount of Jupiter. Again, the Marriage Line comes up from the outer side of the hand under the Mount of the little finger and crosses Mercury. The branches that rise on either side of this clear line are indicative of children. If it drops on to the Line of the Heart, widowhood is likely. If it crosses the Heart Line to the Plain of Mars, this tells of a possible separation, also to be read in the lines of influence that rise on Luna's Mount and go up to the Fate Line. When these touch in both hands, there is a strong likelihood of marriage taking place at that age. But it is the experience of all palmists that an attachment will show as clearly, sometimes more clearly, in the hand of a single person than actual marriage in the hands of frivolous people. Even the cross is occasionally found on the Mount of Jupiter in the hands of lifelong celibates, but it is blurred or marred in some way.